INSIDE!
YOUR MATCH WORLD CUP 2014 BOOK!

KU-098-651

MATCH!

BRAZIL 2014 GUIDE
THE WORLD CUP BOOK FOR FOOTBALL-MAD FANS!

INSIDE! >> 32 Info-Packed Team Guides >> Red-Hot Strikers
>> England Squad Revealed >> Top-Secret Pics & More!

WC 2014 TEAM GUIDES 37

SNAPPED 12

LEGENDS XI 82

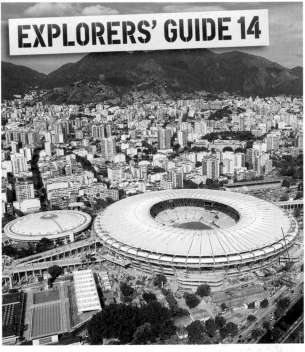

EXPLORERS' GUIDE 14

ENGLAND SQUAD 20

FACT EXPLOSION 30

SUBSCRIBE TO MATCH – TURN TO PAGE 92 FOR MORE INFO!

WELCOME TO THE...
GREATEST SH[O]

The 2014 WORLD CUP in Brazil is nearly here! Check out the reasons why it's going to be truly awesome!

GET READY TO PARTY!

EPIC OPENER!

Holders Spain play Holland in their first game – it's a replay of the red-hot 2010 Final!

MASSIVE GAMES!

We usually have to wait until the knockout stages for heavyweight clashes, but we'll see Germany v Portugal, England v Italy and Spain v Holland in the groups!

BIG STARS!

The tournament will be packed with footy stars! We can't wait to see world-class talent like Lionel Messi, Cristiano Ronaldo, Neymar, Luis Suarez, and Wayne Rooney ripping nets in Brazil!

LEGENDARY HOSTS!

Brazil could be the greatest hosts in World Cup history! The weather will be hot, the fans will be bonkers and the Maracana will be rocking for the final on July 13!

WORLD-CLASS TEAMS!

Some countries have bossed the World Cup over the years, but this could be a really open tournament! Teams like Spain and Argentina look class, while Bosnia-Herzegovina and Chile could be real dark horses!

RONALDO V

The two greatest players on the planet are desperate to own Brazil this summer

> THIS IS RON'S TIME!

WORLD CUP HISTORY!

Ronaldo's World Cup stats are nowhere near as impressive as his La Liga and Champo League numbers for Madrid! He's only bagged two goals and one assist in ten games, but he's a much more complete player in 2014!

RED-HOT FORM!

The Portugal hero heads to Brazil in the best form of his career! He hit 69 goals in 59 games for club and country in 2013 and bagged the Ballon d'Or for the second time! His epic mix of speed, power and ruthlessness is unstoppable!

WHERE THEY COULD MEET!

If Argentina win Group F, Portugal finish runners-up to Germany in Group G and they both win their last 16 games, Ron and Messi will go head-to-head in the quarter-finals!

CRISTIANO RONALDO

Country: Portugal
Club: Real Madrid
Age: 29 **Position:** Winger
World Cups: 2006 & 2010
Boots: Nike Mercurial Vapor IX CR7

HAVIN' A BALL!

The Brazuca is the official Brazil 2014 ball. Check out these all-time classics!

2010
Jabulani

2006
Teamgeist

2002
Fevernova

1998
Tricolore

MESSI!
and stamp their name in World Cup history!

LEO'S GONNA LIGHT UP BRAZIL!

WORLD CUP HISTORY!

Leo's done most things in footy, but he's always struggled at the World Cup - he's grabbed just one goal and two assists in eight games! He was a fresh face in 2006, but his failure to find the net in 2010 was a huge shock!

RED-HOT FORM!

Messi heads to Brazil after the most difficult year of his career! Two big injuries stopped the little genius finding his best form, but he still hit 42 goals in 45 games in all comps! Not bad for someone who's struggled with injuries!

LIONEL MESSI
Country: Argentina
Club: Barcelona
Age: 26 **Position:** Striker
World Cups: 2006 & 2010
Boots: Adidas F50 adizero

GOLDEN BALL!

Check out some of Messi and Ronaldo's rivals for the Player Of The Tournament award!

NEYMAR
BRAZIL

He was Player Of The Tournament at the 2013 Confederations Cup and will be a strong contender again this summer!

ANDRES INIESTA
SPAIN

The reigning champs should have another epic tournament and the Barça magician will be at the heart of all their best moves!

MESUT OZIL
GERMANY

Arsenal's record signing could get loads of votes for the Golden Ball if he fires Germany to glory with his slick skills!

LUIS SUAREZ
URUGUAY

Suarez is ready to stamp his name in footy history after a mind-blowing season with Liverpool! He's unplayable on his day!

FRANCK RIBERY
FRANCE

The whole of France is desperate to see the Bayern Munich wing wizard bring his club form to Les Bleus this summer!

MEET THE MASCOT!

Say hello to World Cup mascot Fuleco, a rock-hard armadillo! You'll be seeing loads of him this summer!

IT'S PARTY TIME!

DID YOU KNOW?

The World Cup trophy was stolen at the 1966 tournament before being found under a hedge in South London by a dog called Pickles!

18 HOLES!
Footy stars love relaxing with a round of golf, so they will be buzzing to hear that the Gavea Golf and Country Club is only a short walk from the hotel!

EXPENSIVE STAY!
The best rooms don't come cheap at the Royal Tulip! It costs a massive £820 to book one of the hotel's king-size suites for just one night!

MATCH GOES INSIDE...

ENGLAND'S HOTEL!

Check out loads of awesome photos, tons of brain-busting facts and all the must-know info about the five-star hotel The Three Lions will be calling home in Brazil this summer!

ROYAL TULIP

FRESH PAINT!
The Royal Tulip is in the middle of a huge upgrade! Millions of pounds are being spent to improve the facilities before England's superstars check in next summer!

PICTURE PERFECT!
England's stars will be able to enjoy epic views of Sao Conrado beach and the giant Gave Stone mountain from their balconies!

THAT MIRROR'S WAY TOO SMALL!

THE BRAZILIAN MASH-UP!
Steven Gerrard + Ronaldinho = GERRARDINHO!

LOL!
Check out Holland heroes Robin van Persie, Wesley Sneijder and Arjen Robben in this cheesy photoshoot 11 years ago! Robben even had hair back then!

COME ON, LET'S PUMP SOME IRON!

LEISURE FACILITIES!
There's a huge leisure area at the hotel with two tennis courts, a huge swimming pool, ultra-modern gym, jewellers, sauna and beauty salon! That should keep the players entertained!

TRAINING GROUND!
England's Urca military training base is a 20-minute drive from their hotel in Sao Conrado! It used to be filled by the Brazilian Army, but now it's an awesome sports centre for travelling teams!

Training ground

England hotel

CRAZY FOOD!
The hotel's two restaurants serve food from around the world. But Feijoada – the local dish containing cow's tongue and pig's feet – is only available at weekends! Shame!

HOTEL FACTPACK!
NAME: Royal Tulip Hotel
LOCATION: Sao Conrado, southern Rio de Janeiro
ROOMS: 418
FLOORS: 17
STAR RATING: 5
FAB FACT: England have booked the hotel until after the World Cup final. That's how confident gaffer Roy Hodgson is in his squad!

LEARN THE LINGO!
The locals in Brazil speak Portuguese, so check out these footy phrases!

Hello | Olá
Translate

English	Portuguese
I love football!	Eu amo o futebol!
Awesome goal!	Incrivel meta!
Red card!	Cartao vermelho!
Man of the match!	Homem do jogo!
You're having a laugh, ref!	Voce esta tendo uma risada, arbitro!
Sort it out, gaffer!	Resolver o problema, o gerente!
Get Rickie Lambert on the pitch!	Obter Rickie Lambert em campo!
Your striker is slower than a tortoise!	O atacante e mais lento que uma tartaruga!
You only sing when you're winning!	Voce so cantar quando voce esta ganhando!

OLA, WAZZA!

EH?!?!

SCARECUTS!
Stephan El Shaarawy, Italy

HAMMERS HEROES!
West Ham had three stars in England's 1966 World Cup winning team – Geoff Hurst, Martin Peters and Bobby Moore! Hurst's hat-trick sunk West Germany in the final!

ALL EYES ON NEYMAR!

Over 200 million Brazilians expect NEYMAR to lead the Samba Stars to World Cup 2014 glory! MATCH checks out the reasons why he can be the star of the summer!

SLICK TRICKS!
Nobody in world footy busts out more tricks than the Barça legend! He makes defenders look stupid with his flash flip-flaps, rabonas, stepovers and loads more!

MEGA CONFIDENCE!
Neymar will love being in the spotlight this summer, because he's so confident! He's got tons of sponsorship deals, including Nike and Police sunglasses, and he's always posing on Instagram!

ZLATAN'S SAD SUMMER!

GOT ANY SUN CREAM, MATE?

Zlatan Ibrahimovic has plenty of time to top up his tan this summer after Sweden got dumped out in the play-offs!

CRAZY FACES!

WE'RE TOTALLY BONKERS, MATCH!

Check out these mad Colombia fans! They might get a bit warm in Brazil this summer!

LETHAL FINISHING!

Neymar's main strengths were dribbling and tricks when he was younger, but his one-on-one finishing and long-shots have improved big-time! He's netted 27 goals in 46 games for Brazil!

RECORD CHASER!

Miroslav Klose needs just one goal to overtake Ronaldo as the World Cup's all-time top scorer!

WORLD CUP 2002
5 GOALS

The Germany star became the first player ever to bag five headed goals in a World Cup!

WORLD CUP 2006
5 GOALS

Germany hosted the World Cup in 2006 and Klose was their star striker again with five more goals!

WORLD CUP 2010
4 GOALS

He was 32 at the last World Cup but still managed to score four goals, including a double against Argentina!

TOTAL: 14 GOALS

PLEASE DON'T STEAL MY RECORD!

CONFEDERATIONS CUP CLASS!

He bagged the Golden Ball at last summer's Confederations Cup! His four goals also helped Brazil win the trophy!

BATTLE FOR DRAXLER!

Gossips reckon Prem giants Arsenal, Chelsea and Man. United will scrap it out for Germany wonderkid Julian Draxler after the World Cup!

WORLD CUP FACE PALM!

Is it just us, or does the official 2014 logo look like a huge face palm?

THAT'S ONE RUBBISH LOGO!

SNAPPED!

MATCH checks out the best pics from the World Cup qualifiers!

Haircut battle!

So that's why Lukaku cut his hair off – he lost the showdown to Axel Witsel!

HANDS UP IF YOU LIKE MINE BETTER!

Mega fart attack!

Yohan Cabaye busts out his trademark quadro-guff move!

FOUR SWEET PUMPS COMING YOUR WAY!

Samba dance-off!

The Brazil boys get competitive when it comes to dancing!

WE'RE BETTER THAN STURRIDGE!

LET ME HAVE SOME!

That's no World Cup, it's a giant Ferrero Rocher!

BRAZIL 2014...
EXPLORERS' GUIDE!

MATCH reveals everything you need to know about the 2014 World Cup host cities!

AMAZONIA ARENA

Capacity: 42,374
Building work: New stadium
Biggest match: England v Italy

MANAUS

NICKNAME:
The Paris Of The Tropics
POPULATION: 2 million
BIGGEST CLUB: Nacional
LOCAL LEGEND: Cristiano
AVERAGE JUNE TEMP: 26°C

CUIABA

NICKNAME: The Green City
POPULATION: 940,000
BIGGEST CLUB: Mixto Sports Club
LOCAL LEGEND: Vandinho
AVERAGE JUNE TEMP: 24°C

PANTANAL ARENA

Capacity: 42,968
Building work: New stadium
Biggest match: Japan v Colombia

SALVADOR

NICKNAME:
The Capital Of Happiness
POPULATION: 2.6 million
BIGGEST CLUB: Bahia Sports Club
LOCAL LEGEND: Dante
AVERAGE JUNE TEMP: 24°C

The Amazon River is surrounded by the world's biggest rainforest, which is home to over 10 million species of plants and animals including jaguars, monkeys, sloths and capybara!

The Amazon River is over 4,000 miles long, and three quarters of it is found in Brazil! Adventurers travel to study its 3,000 different species of fish, piranha and giant anacondas!

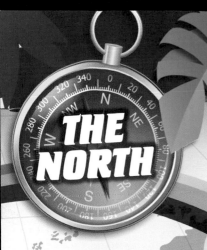

THE NORTH

CASTELAO STADIUM

Capacity: 64,846
Building work: Massive upgrade
Biggest match: Quarter-final

FORTALEZA

NICKNAME: Fortal
POPULATION: 2.5 million
BIGGEST CLUB: Ceara Sporting Club
LOCAL LEGEND: Mario Jardel
AVERAGE JUNE TEMP: 26°C

NATAL

NICKNAME: The City Of The Sun
POPULATION: 950,000
BIGGEST CLUB: America de Natal
LOCAL LEGEND: Matuzalem
AVERAGE JUNE TEMP: 26°C

DAS DUNAS ARENA

Capacity: 42,086
Building work: New stadium
Biggest match: Italy v Uruguay

Brazil is packed with awesome animals, but the Brazilian Wandering Spider is definitely one to avoid! It's the world's deadliest spider with a bite that can kill a human in just 25 minutes!

RECIFE

NICKNAME: Brazilian Venice
POPULATION: 1.5 million
BIGGEST CLUB: Sport Recife
LOCAL LEGEND: Rivaldo
AVERAGE JUNE TEMP: 25°C

FONTE NOVA ARENA

Capacity: 52,048
Building work: Massive upgrade
Biggest match: Quarter-final

PERNAMBUCO ARENA

Capacity: 44,248
Building work: New stadium
Biggest match: Last 16

One of Brazil's greatest tourist attractions is a cool system of 275-linked waterfalls on the Iguazu River! The most famous waterfall in the system is an 82-metre high U-shaped drop called The Devil's Throat!

MINEIRAO STADIUM

Capacity: 62,547
Building work: Massive upgrade
Biggest match: Semi-final

BELO HORIZONTE

NICKNAME: The Garden City
POPULATION: 2.4 million
BIGGEST CLUB: Cruzeiro
LOCAL LEGEND: Bernard
AVERAGE JUNE TEMP: 19°C

BRASILIA

NICKNAME: Capital Of Hope
POPULATION: 2.8 million
BIGGEST CLUB: Brasiliense
LOCAL LEGEND: Kaka
AVERAGE JUNE TEMP: 19°C

MANE GARRINCHA STADIUM

Capacity: 68,009
Building work: Complete rebuild
Biggest match: Quarter-final

SAO PAULO ARENA

Capacity: 65,807
Building work: New stadium
Biggest match: Semi-final

SAO PAULO

NICKNAME: Land Of Drizzle
POPULATION: 11.3 million
BIGGEST CLUB: Corinthians
LOCAL LEGEND: Robinho
AVERAGE JUNE TEMP: 16°C

The Pantanal in the west of Brazil is one of the world's biggest swamps! It covers around 75,000 square miles and is home to giant anacondas, alligators, wolves, anteaters and millions of lethal Yacare Caiman!

MARACANA STADIUM

Capacity: 76,804
Building work: Massive upgrade
Biggest match: Final

RIO DE JANEIRO

NICKNAME: Rio
POPULATION: 6.3 million
BIGGEST CLUB: Flamengo
LOCAL LEGEND: Ronaldo
AVERAGE JUNE TEMP: 23°C

N
NE
S

THE SOUTH

Beto Carrero World in eastern Brazil is the largest theme park in South America! It's a five-square-mile park with seven rollercoasters, three water rides, tons of shows and a zoo!

CURITIBA

NICKNAME:
The City Of Eternal Fog
POPULATION: 1.7 million
BIGGEST CLUB:
Atletico Paranaense
LOCAL LEGEND: Adriano
AVERAGE JUNE TEMP:
12°C

DA BAIXADA ARENA

Capacity: 41,456
Building work: Massive upgrade
Biggest match: Australia v Spain

Probably the most famous tourist attraction in Brazil is the 39-metre tall statue of Jesus, which overlooks Rio de Janeiro! Millions of footy fans will queue up to get snapped in front of Christ The Redeemer in 2014!

BEIRA-RIO STADIUM

Capacity: 50,287
Building work: Massive upgrade
Biggest match: Last 16

PORTO ALEGRE

NICKNAME: The Valiant City
POPULATION: 1.5 million
BIGGEST CLUB: Gremio
LOCAL LEGEND: Ronaldinho
AVERAGE JUNE TEMP:
15°C

The world's biggest and most famous party is held on the streets of Rio de Janeiro every year! The Rio Carnival attracts two million people a day onto the streets of Brazil's second city for mad singing and dancing!

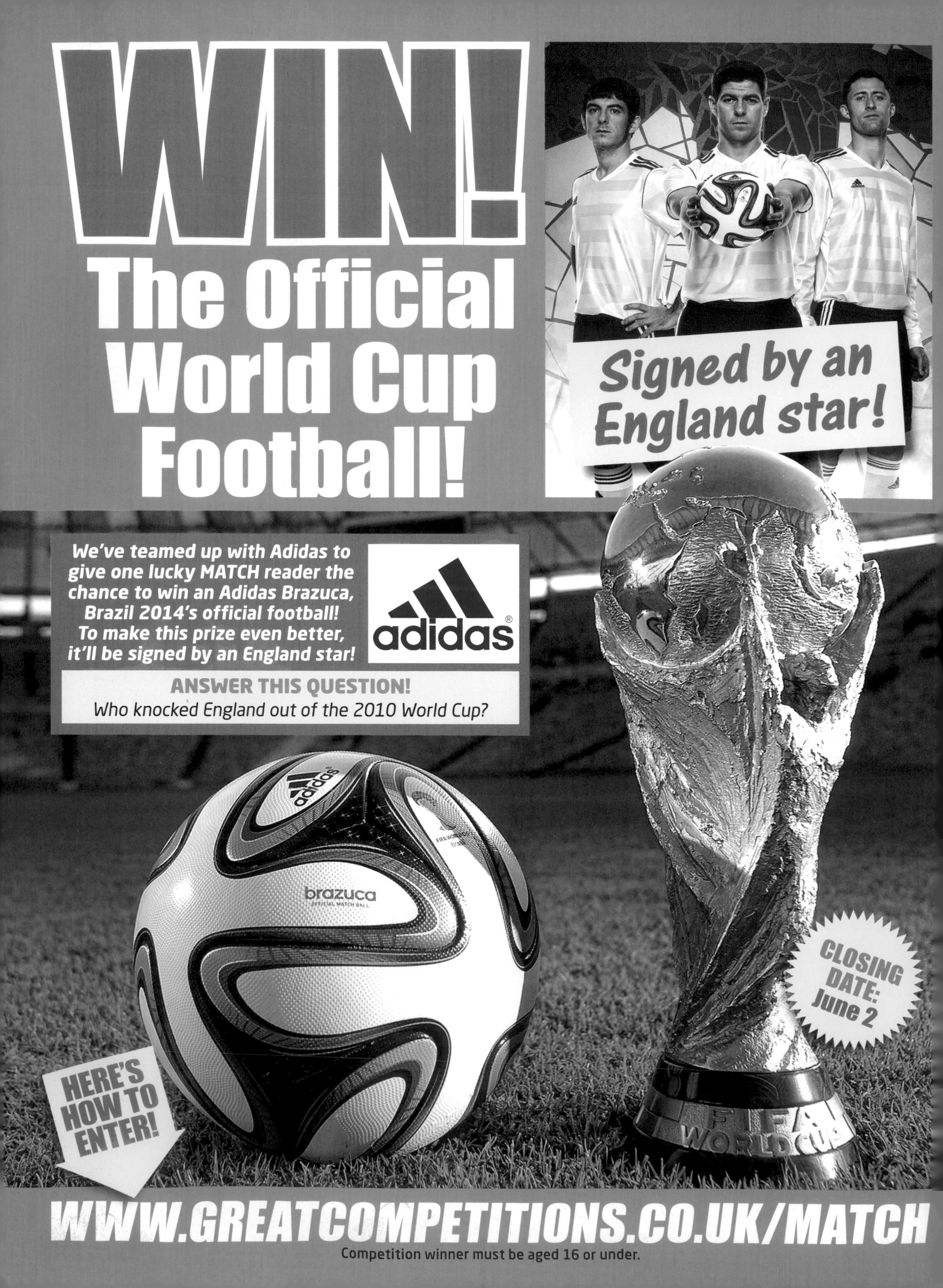

WIN!

The Official World Cup Football!

Signed by an England star!

We've teamed up with Adidas to give one lucky MATCH reader the chance to win an Adidas Brazuca, Brazil 2014's official football! To make this prize even better, it'll be signed by an England star!

adidas

ANSWER THIS QUESTION!
Who knocked England out of the 2010 World Cup?

brazuca
OFFICIAL MATCH BALL

HERE'S HOW TO ENTER!

CLOSING DATE: June 2

WWW.GREATCOMPETITIONS.CO.UK/MATCH

Competition winner must be aged 16 or under.

NEYMAR

BRAZIL

He won the FIFA Goal Of The Year award in 2011 for a dribble and strike for Santos against Flamengo. He was only 19 at the time!

Neymar scored four goals in five games and was named Player Of The Tournament at last summer's Confederations Cup in Brazil!

The lethal striker bagged an epic 136 goals in 225 appearances for Santos before moving to Barcelona last summer!

ENGLAND'S ULTIMATE 23!

MATCH's footy experts pick the squad Roy Hodgson SHOULD be taking to Brazil!

ENGLAND

THE WINNING FORMULA!

England's best chance of winning the World Cup is to play to our strengths - that's fast, power-packed, all or nothing football! We've picked the best English squad to do that, with a handful of different attacking options to allow us to change our playing style and formation off the bench!

BEN FOSTER
Club: West Brom Age: 31

READO SAYS: "Fozzie gets ignored because he's hidden in mid-table with The Baggies, but he's a top-class keeper. Like Hart he's had a couple of slips this season, but his ability to make wonder saves combined with the way he dominates his penalty box means he's a solid back-up to Hart!"

JOE HART
Club: Man. City Age: 26

ROCKET SAYS: "Hart's got tons of stick for a couple of mistakes he's made this season, but there's no doubt he's still England's first-choice keeper! His shot-stopping is immense, his positioning is flawless, and he always delivers when it comes to the big matches!"

FRASER FORSTER
Club: Celtic Age: 26

STEVO SAYS: "Forster kept 11 clean sheets in a row in the SPL earlier this season, and his epic shot-stopping was a big reason for that. He's also shown he has the confidence and class to go toe-to-toe with the world's top strikers in the Champions League!"

GLEN JOHNSON
Club: Liverpool **Age:** 29

PHIL JONES
Club: Man. United **Age:** 22

ROCKET SAYS: "We're only naming seven defenders in our squad, so we need a utility player to cover two positions, and Jones is that man. The Red Devils' youngster hasn't had his best season, but he's still a quality centre-back who can cover at right-back, or even midfield, if injuries strike!"

READO SAYS: "Johnson would definitely be in our first XI. He's fast, an excellent crosser and has the technique to score wondergoals with both feet! But most importantly, his positioning and footy brain have improved recently, so his defending has got loads better too!"

PHIL JAGIELKA
Club: Everton **Age:** 31

READO SAYS: "Jags has been rock-solid for Everton this season and would be a guaranteed starter in Brazil. Some experts don't give The Toffees' captain the respect he deserves, but he reads the game like a legend, is quick across the ground and times his tackles perfectly!"

GARY CAHILL
Club: Chelsea **Age:** 28

STEVO SAYS: "England need their players to deliver big performances in huge matches at the World Cup, and that's exactly what Cahill's been doing this season. He's also formed a solid partnership with Jagielka and impressed when playing against Luis Suarez, which should come in handy too!"

JOLEON LESCOTT
Club: Man. City **Age:** 31

ROCKET SAYS: "Lescott hasn't been a regular for City this season and has been out of the picture for England recently, but we think that's a mistake! The City ace is a quality penalty box defender with awesome pace and heading ability, and would give great cover at centre-back!"

LEIGHTON BAINES
Club: Everton Age: 29

STEVO SAYS: "Bainesy has cemented his place as England's first-choice left-back in the last year and we wouldn't dream of changing that! The flying Evertonian is a solid defender, but his attacking runs, whipped crosses, thunderbolt free-kicks and lethal penalties would win matches too!"

ASHLEY COLE
Club: Chelsea Age: 33

READO SAYS: "Cole wouldn't be an automatic starter in our team, but he'd be a key member of the squad! The Blues' legend is still one of the world's very best left-backs and his experience, clever runs and excellent man-marking would give us great options down the left side!"

MICHAEL CARRICK
Club: Man. United Age: 32

ROCKET SAYS: "Carrick wouldn't start many matches, but he'd still be a key part of our plans in Brazil. The Man. United anchorman's footy brain and passing skills mean he can sit in front of the defence and squeeze the life out of the opposition in the second half. A great option to have when you're 1-0 up!"

STEVEN GERRARD
Club: Liverpool Age: 33

READO SAYS: "England need a holding midfielder to protect the defence, and we wouldn't want anyone other than Stevie G to do that job! The skipper hasn't got the legs to burst from box-to-box these days, but his rapid footy brain and eye for a pass mean he's the perfect man to start off attacks!"

JACK WILSHERE
Club: Arsenal Age: 22

STEVO SAYS: "Jack would be our pick as Gerrard's midfield partner, if he can hit top form before June. His low centre of gravity gives him the balance to roll tackles and run into space before picking a pass to open up the opposition. He's a pure competitor and his clever one-twos will win matches!"

ROSS BARKLEY
Club: Everton Age: 20

READO SAYS: "Barkley's shown he can dominate the biggest matches over the last year, and we reckon that can continue in Brazil! The 20 year old's favourite position is taken by Wayne Rooney, but Ross can slot in across the midfield, and has the skills and confidence to transform a match off the subs' bench!"

JORDAN HENDERSON
Club: Liverpool Age: 23

ROCKET SAYS: "Frank Lampard had one foot in MATCH's England squad until Henderson nicked his place at the last minute! The midfielder has been excellent for The Reds this season, breaking up play and launching attacks. He doesn't give opponents an inch, and that could be vital against Uruguay and Italy!"

RAHEEM STERLING
Club: Liverpool Age: 19

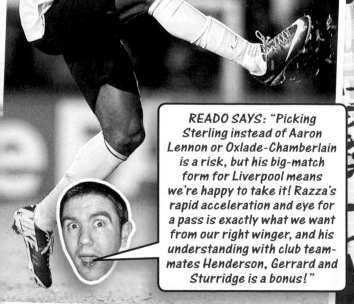

READO SAYS: "Picking Sterling instead of Aaron Lennon or Oxlade-Chamberlain is a risk, but his big-match form for Liverpool means we're happy to take it! Razza's rapid acceleration and eye for a pass is exactly what we want from our right winger, and his understanding with club team-mates Henderson, Gerrard and Sturridge is a bonus!"

ANDROS TOWNSEND
Club: Tottenham Age: 22

STEVO SAYS: "Andros booked his World Cup place when he tore Poland and Montenegro to pieces last year! But the Spurs speedster's been almost invisible since then and would need to prove he still has the confidence, pace and goal threat in England training to be our first-choice right winger in Brazil!"

JAMES MILNER
Club: Man. City Age: 28

READO SAYS: "Milner's one of the most underrated players in England. He hit almost 20 goals in a season for Aston Villa a few years ago, and creates just as many chances for his team-mates! He's got a top footy brain, has one of the best whipped crosses in the England squad and runs all day for his team-mates!"

ADAM LALLANA
Club: Southampton Age: 25

ROCKET SAYS: "The Saints' captain has played his way into the squad this season and impressed in the friendlies against Chile and Germany! He has bags of confidence, links up brilliantly with the strikers and creates loads of chances by running at the opposition. He's also proved he can chip in with big goals at key moments this season!"

WAYNE ROONEY
Club: Man. United Age: 28

READO SAYS: "Wazza is England's most dangerous player, so we'd build our team, formation and tactics around getting him the ball! The Man. United superstar is an unstoppable force in the hole behind the lead striker, from where his last-minute runs, inch-perfect through-balls and net-ripping long-shots win matches!"

DANIEL STURRIDGE
Club: Liverpool Age: 24

STEVO SAYS: "MATCH first interviewed Studger when he was just 16 years old, and we knew then that he'd go on to star for The Three Lions! He's lightning fast, hits screamers from distance, has awesome footwork and always seems to pop up in the right place at the right time to score! We can't wait to see him linking up with Rooney!"

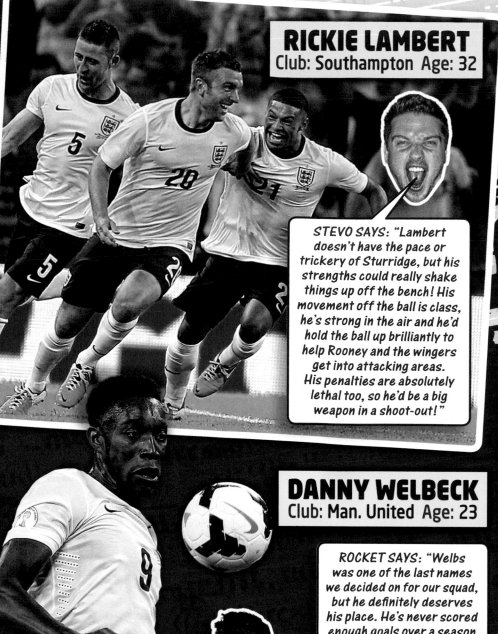

RICKIE LAMBERT
Club: Southampton **Age:** 32

STEVO SAYS: "Lambert doesn't have the pace or trickery of Sturridge, but his strengths could really shake things up off the bench! His movement off the ball is class, he's strong in the air and he'd hold the ball up brilliantly to help Rooney and the wingers get into attacking areas. His penalties are absolutely lethal too, so he'd be a big weapon in a shoot-out!"

DANNY WELBECK
Club: Man. United **Age:** 23

ROCKET SAYS: "Welbs was one of the last names we decided on for our squad, but he definitely deserves his place. He's never scored enough goals over a season for his club, but his England goals to games record has always been around the one in two mark. He leads the line well, moves defenders around like a ledge and can play on the left-wing too!"

THE DREAM 23!
Check out MATCH's ultimate England squad for Brazil 2014!

GOALKEEPERS

		Caps	Clean Sheets
1.	JOE HART	38	16
13.	BEN FOSTER	6	2
23.	FRASER FORSTER	1	0

DEFENDERS

		Caps	Goals
2.	GLEN JOHNSON	49	1
3.	LEIGHTON BAINES	22	1
5.	PHIL JAGIELKA	24	1
6.	GARY CAHILL	21	2
12.	PHIL JONES	9	0
14.	JOLEON LESCOTT	26	1
15.	ASHLEY COLE	106	0

MIDFIELDERS

		Caps	Goals
4.	STEVEN GERRARD	108	21
7.	ANDROS TOWNSEND	4	1
8.	JACK WILSHERE	14	0
11.	ADAM LALLANA	2	0
16.	MICHAEL CARRICK	31	0
17.	ROSS BARKLEY	3	0
18.	JORDAN HENDERSON	7	0
19.	RAHEEM STERLING	1	0
20.	JAMES MILNER	44	1

STRIKERS

		Caps	Goals
9.	DANIEL STURRIDGE	9	2
10.	WAYNE ROONEY	88	38
21.	RICKIE LAMBERT	4	2
22.	DANNY WELBECK	20	8

ON STANDBY

JOHN RUDDY, Norwich

CURTIS DAVIES, Hull

FRANK LAMPARD, Chelsea

ALEX OXLADE-CHAMBERLAIN, Arsenal

JAY RODRIGUEZ, Southampton

All caps, goals and clean sheet stats correct up to...

IS ANYBODY MISSING?

There are two players missing from MATCH's England 23 that we'd have loved to include. **John Terry** has probably been the best centre-back in the Prem this season, but Chelsea's legendary captain has retired from international football! Arsenal's **Theo Walcott** would've been a key player in our England team too, but his nasty knee injury against Tottenham rules him out!

SQUAD TALK!
Visit the MATCH Facebook page at 4pm on May 20 and June 6 to talk to the MATCH experts about who you would have in your England 23!

RICKIE LAMBERT'S...
BRAZIL BUZZ!

The ENGLAND and SOUTHAMPTON hero chats about the excitement of this summer's World Cup!

Squad place race!

RICKIE SAYS: "It feels absolutely unbelievable to have a chance of playing in a World Cup, especially when you think I was playing in League 1 four years ago! But I'm very focused on what I need to try to do to get there, and that's doing well for Southampton!"

Group D's really tough!

RICKIE SAYS: "It's a very, very hard draw. But it's the World Cup, so that's how every team is! It's tough, but not impossible, so we've got to be confident. I feel that if we perform, we can get through to the second round."

I really struggled watching the draw!

RICKIE SAYS: "I watched the draw at my house. I had my kids with me, so I had to keep turning on kids' TV every five minutes to keep them happy, then turn back to see if the draw had happened!"

Gaston has got loads of banter!

RICKIE SAYS: "I didn't speak to Adam Lallana or Jay Rodriguez after the draw, because I knew that I was seeing everyone for pre-match the next day. All the lads made jokes to Gaston Ramirez about Uruguay – just a bit of banter – but it was funny!"

Osvaldo's had a goal warning!

RICKIE SAYS: "Dani Osvaldo scored a great goal against Man. City in the match after the draw, and I told him he'd better not do that against us! It's good banter, but if I get the chance to go to the World Cup, it will be nice to see him and Gaston there!"

I'm ready for penalties!

RICKIE SAYS: "I see a penalty as being as simple as anything you'll have to deal with in your career. It's a free shot from 12 yards, so you should score and I'm always confident I will. If you try to complicate it you're only helping the keeper, so I don't!"

"IT FEELS UNBELIEVABLE TO HAVE A CHANCE OF PLAYING IN A WORLD CUP!"

RU 2 BROTHERS?

Check out these crazy World Cup lookalikes!

EDUARDO
CROATIA

ZAYN
ONE DIRECTION

BIG BIRD
SESAME STREET

MAROUANE FELLAINI
BELGIUM

CHRIS SMALLING
ENGLAND

EMELI SANDE
SINGER

NEYMAR
BRAZIL

BARACK OBAMA
USA PRESIDENT

LUIS SUAREZ
URUGUAY

SID THE SLOTH
ICE AGE

SIDESHOW BOB
THE SIMPSONS

DAVID LUIZ
BRAZIL

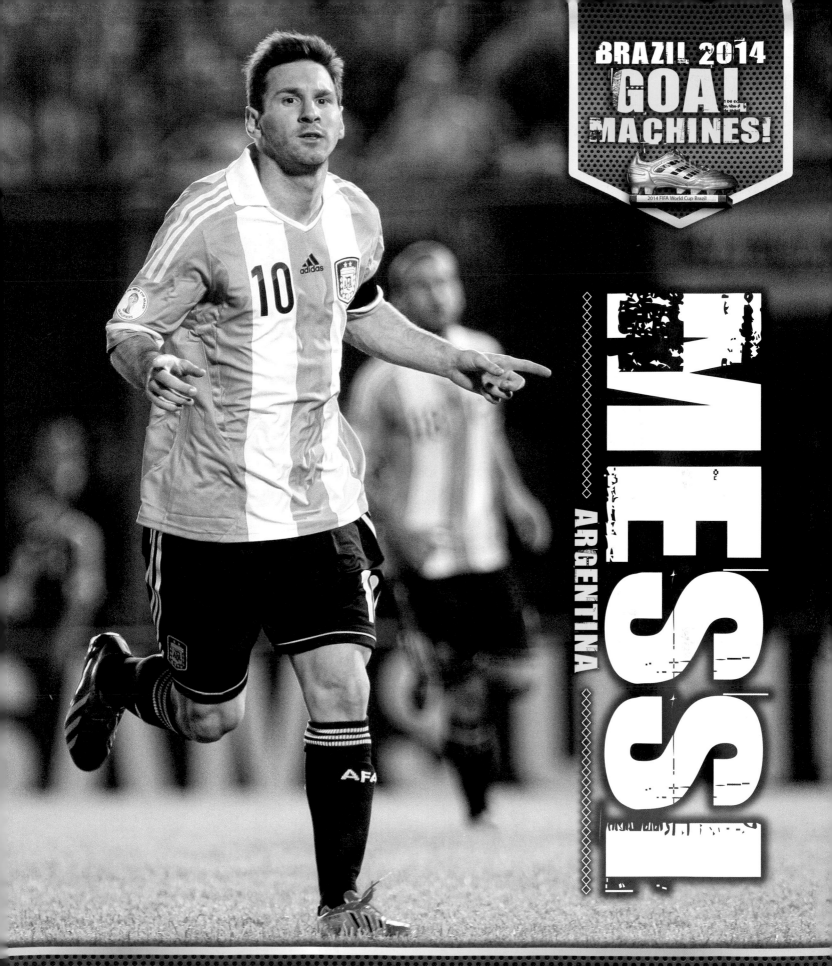

MESSI

ARGENTINA

The Argentina genius is the only player in history to win the Ballon d'Or and Champions League top scorer prizes four years in a row!

Messi bagged 42 goals in just 45 games for Barcelona and Argentina in 2013, even though he picked up two big injuries!

He netted 50 La Liga goals in 2011-12, which was the highest winning total in the history of the European Golden Boot! Legend!

WORLD CUP FACT EXPL

5

South American legends Brazil have won the World Cup five times – that's more than any other country!

1930

Uruguay won the first ever World Cup back in 1930! Can Luis Suarez help them do it again?

3

England and Italy share the record for most World Cup penalty shoot-out defeats – they've lost three each!

1

Only one of the 32 teams in Brazil will be playing in their first World Cup – Bosnia & Herzegovina!

30

Germany have scored the most goals at the last two World Cup tournaments! They bagged 16 in 2010 and 14 in 2006!

28

The 2006 World Cup was the dirtiest ever, with 28 red cards in 64 games!

OSION!

20

This year's hosts Brazil are the only country to have played in all 20 World Cup tournaments!

13

France's Just Fontaine holds the record for hitting the most goals in a single World Cup tournament – he scored 13 in 1958!

16

A crazy 16 cards were shown during Portugal's fiery clash with Holland at the 2006 World Cup, with four players sent off!

199,854

That's how many fans watched Brazil play Uruguay at the Maracana Stadium in 1950! That's the highest attendance in World Cup history!

171

Dennis Bergkamp, Zinedine Zidane and Ronaldo helped make the 1998 tournament the highest-scoring finals ever, when 171 goals were scored in France!

10

Turkey's Hakan Sukur hit the quickest goal in World Cup history when he netted after 10.89 seconds against South Korea in 2002!

4

No country has lost more World Cup finals than Germany! They've won three, but lost FOUR!

3

Pele is the only player in footy history to have won the World Cup three times! He lifted the trophy in 1958, 1962 and 1970!

1966

England won their only World Cup back in 1966! Geoff Hurst hit a hat-trick against West Germany in the final – the only ever World Cup final treble!

2

The World Cup final has been decided by a penalty shoot-out twice! Brazil beat Italy in 1994 and Italy stunned France in 2006!

15

Brazil icon Ronaldo is the highest scorer in World Cup history, with 15 goals between 1998 and 2006!

6

World Cups have been won by the host nation six times, including France back in 1998!

BIG MATCH! QUIZ

WORLD CUP SPECIAL!

CAMERA SHY!

Name the World Cup megastars hiding from the snappers in these cool pics!

BOGUS BADGE!

Do you know which massive World Cup country this cool badge belongs to?

BONKERS FANS!

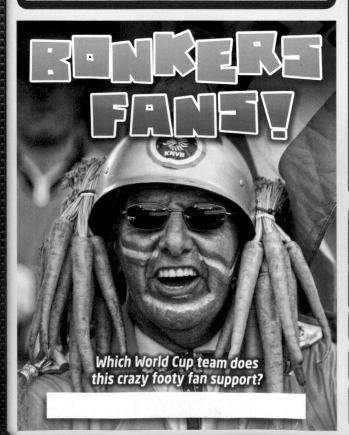

Which World Cup team does this crazy footy fan support?

WORLD CUP HEROES!

A Belgium

B Ecuador

C Nigeria

Match these World Cup stars to the countries they play for!

Victor Moses **1**

Kevin Mirallas **2**

Antonio Valencia **3**

WHO AM I?

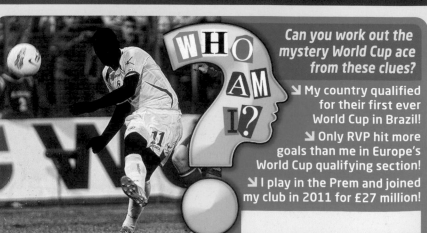

Can you work out the mystery World Cup ace from these clues?

↘ My country qualified for their first ever World Cup in Brazil!

↘ Only RVP hit more goals than me in Europe's World Cup qualifying section!

↘ I play in the Prem and joined my club in 2011 for £27 million!

NAME THE TEAM!

ANSWERS ON PAGE 90

Can you remember England's XI that beat Poland 2-0 to seal World Cup qualification?

1. Liverpool ★ Striker

2. Man. United ★ Winger

3. Everton ★ Centre-back

4. Man. City ★ Goalkeeper

5. Chelsea ★ Centre-back

Man. United ★ Right-back
CHRIS SMALLING

6. Tottenham ★ Winger

7. Man. United ★ Striker

8. Liverpool ★ Midfielder

9. Man. United ★ Midfielder

10. Everton ★ Left-back

2014 FIFA WORLD CUP BRAZIL™ QUALIFIERS
ENGLAND v POLAND
TUESDAY 15 OCTOBER 2013, WEMBLEY STADIUM

VAUXHALL
THE ENGLAND TEAM SPONSOR

150 YEARS of The FA

FOOTY CRAZY!

Can you name the World Cup finals these epic footies were used at?

1. Teamgeist

2. Brazuca

3. Jabulani

4. Fevernova

MYSTERY MASCOT!

Name the World Cup host country this mascot is from using these clues!

↘ My name is Footix and I was mascot for the 1998 World Cup!

↘ I was massive mates with Youri, Thierry, Zinedine and Emmanuel!

↘ My country was the last World Cup hosts to win the tournament!

FLASHBACK!

Which World Cup legend will want to forget this dodgy old pic?

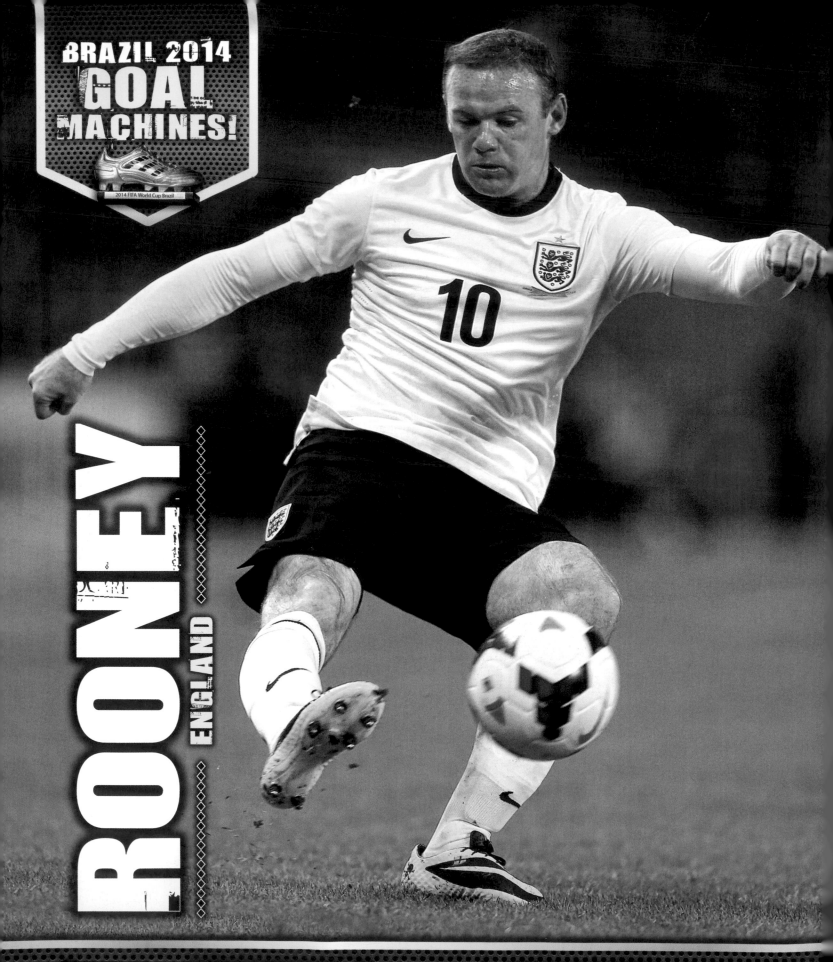

ROONEY
ENGLAND

Rooney was The Three Lions' top scorer in World Cup qualifying with seven goals in just six matches in Group H! What a legend!

Wazza was named in UEFA's Team Of The Tournament after bursting onto the scene with four goals in four games at Euro 2004!

He became only the fourth player to score 200 goals for Man. United when he bagged a double against Bayer Leverkusen last September!

GROUP A | **PAGE 38**

GROUP B | **PAGE 42**

GROUP C | **PAGE 48**

BRAZIL 2014 TEAM GUIDES

GROUP D | **PAGE 52**

GROUP E | **PAGE 58**

GROUP F | **PAGE 62**

GROUP G | **PAGE 68**

GROUP H | **PAGE 72**

MATCH looks at the star man, wonderkid, strengths, weaknesses, strongest XI and all of the must-know stats for every one of the 32 World Cup teams!

All world rankings, results, caps and goal stats correct up to Feb. 13, 2014.

BRAZIL

COACH	LUIZ FELIPE SCOLARI	CAPTAIN	THIAGO SILVA	MOST CAPS	ROBINHO 92

WARM-UP FORM!

As World Cup hosts, Brazil didn't need to worry about qualifying for this tournament! Instead they've been travelling the world teaching teams like Portugal, Chile and South Korea a few footballing lessons in friendlies! Their biggest test came last summer in the Confederations Cup where, after beating Japan, Italy, Mexico and Uruguay, they totally outplayed Spain in the final to prove they're title contenders!

THE TACTICS!

Brazil play a 4-2-3-1 system with the focus on their speedy full-backs carrying the ball forward as quickly as they can. Dani Alves and Marcelo's runs create tons of space for Hulk, Oscar and Neymar who produce the magic around the penalty box!

Dani Alves

STRENGTH!

Brazil have tons of goalscoring threats from the edge of the box with Neymar's movement, Hulk's direct play and Oscar's long shots!

WEAKNESS!

The full-backs can bomb forward too much and leave big holes in their defence when they push upfield!

STAR MAN!

NEYMAR
BARCELONA

CAPS: 46 **GOALS:** 27

Barcelona emptied every bank in Spain to sign Neymar last summer, and he's been worth every single penny! The Samba superstar has great awareness, beats players with ease and makes opponents look like fools with his epic tricks! He scores every kind of goal, too!

WATCH OUT FOR...

BERNARD
SHAKHTAR DONETSK

CAPS: 10 **GOALS:** 1

Bernard is so small that he sometimes gets lost on the Brazil team coach, but he's as fast as lightning! The winger loves driving at full-backs with the ball at his feet and could be Brazil's super sub!

LAST FIVE RESULTS!

Sep. 10 2013	**Brazil** Thiago Silva 23, Neymar 34, Jo 49	**3-1**	**Portugal** Meireles 17
Oct. 12 2013	**South Korea**	**0-2**	**Brazil** Neymar 44, Oscar 49
Oct. 15 2013	**Brazil** Oscar 59, Dede 66	**2-0**	**Zambia**
Nov. 16 2013	**Honduras**	**0-5**	**Brazil** Bernard 22, Dante 55, Maicon 66, Willian 70, Hulk 74
Nov. 19 2013	**Brazil** Hulk 14, Robinho 79	**2-1**	**Chile** Vargas 71

STRONGEST STARTING XI!

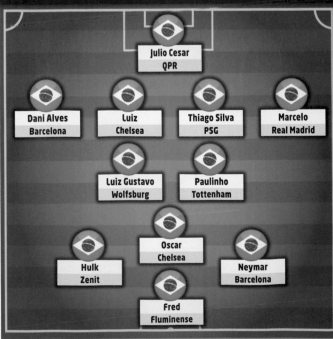

Julio Cesar
QPR

Dani Alves
Barcelona

Luiz
Chelsea

Thiago Silva
PSG

Marcelo
Real Madrid

Luiz Gustavo
Wolfsburg

Paulinho
Tottenham

Oscar
Chelsea

Hulk
Zenit

Neymar
Barcelona

Fred
Fluminense

SUPER SUBS: Jefferson, Cavalieri, Maicon, Dante, Miranda, Maxwell, Ramires, Hernanes, Lucas Moura, Bernard, Robinho, Jo.

BRAZIL'S HEROES!

PENALTY KING
Fred

SPEED MACHINE
Thiago Silva

MUSCLEMAN
Dante

WONDERKID
Neymar

MATCH VERDICT!

The hosts' balance of lethal attacking talent and rapid defenders mean they're the World Cup favourites, but we think the pressure to perform on home soil could see them crash out in the semi-finals!

CROATIA

COACH NIKO KOVAC	**WORLD RANKING** 16TH	**WORLD CUP ODDS** 125/1	**WORLD CUP BEST** THIRD PLACE 1998

QUALIFYING FORM!

Croatia made a flying start to qualifying with big results against Serbia and Belgium! But their form fell apart in 2013, and they only just finished as Group A runners-up! Niko Kovac replaced Igor Stimac as manager for the play-offs, where they beat Iceland 2-0 on aggregate!

Ivan Rakitic

STRENGTH!

Croatia's midfield is loaded with skilful, quick players and Mario Mandzukic is a class lone striker!

WEAKNESS!

Croatia's centre-backs will struggle against rapid strikers and keeper Stipe Pletikosa is way past his best!

LAST FIVE RESULTS!

Sep. 13 2013	South Korea Keun-Ho Lee 90	1-2	Croatia Vida 65, N. Kalinic 71
Oct. 11 2013	Croatia Kranjcar 83	1-2	Belgium Lukaku 15, 38
Oct. 15 2013	Scotland Snodgrass 29, Naismith 73	2-0	Croatia
Nov. 15 2013	Iceland	0-0	Croatia
Nov. 19 2013	Croatia Mandzukic 27, Srna 47	2-0	Iceland

STAR MAN!

LUKA MODRIC
REAL MADRID

Caps: 72 **Goals:** 8

Croatia's midfield master doesn't look like your normal footballer. He's skinny, pale and barely has an ounce of muscle, but you'd be a fool to underestimate him! He has a quick brain, great passing skills and loses his marker so easily!

STRONGEST STARTING XI!

Pletikosa — Rostov

Srna — Shakhtar
Corluka — L. Moscow
Simunic — Dinamo Zagreb
Strinic — Dnipro

Rakitic — Sevilla
Kovacic — Inter Milan
Modric — Real Madrid

Perisic — Wolfsburg
Olic — Wolfsburg

Mandzukic — Bayern Munich

SUPER SUBS: Subasic, L. Kalinic, Vrsaljko, Lovren, Schildenfeld, Pranjic, Males, Badelj, Ilicevic, Rebic, Eduardo, Jelavic.

CROATIA'S HEROES!

 PENALTY KING Ivan Rakitic

 SPEED MACHINE Ivan Rakitic

 MUSCLEMAN Vedran Corluka

 WONDERKID Mateo Kovacic

MATCH VERDICT!

If goal king Mandzukic wasn't banned for Croatia's opener against hosts Brazil a shock might have been on! But he is, so Croatia should take the runners-up spot before losing to Spain in the second round!

MEXICO

| COACH | MIGUEL HERRERA | WORLD RANKING | 21ST | WORLD CUP ODDS | 100/1 | WORLD CUP BEST | QUARTER-FINALS 1970 & 1986 |

QUALIFYING FORM!

Mexico were terrible in qualifying, winning only two of their ten group matches! But the USA's last-second win against Panama meant Mexico bagged a play-off against New Zealand, which they won to qualify!

STAR MAN! Oribe Peralta

STRENGTH!

The core of the starting XI play for Mexican League giants America, so they know each other inside out!

WEAKNESS!

Mexico's defence is way short on pace, so they can be opened up when the wing-backs push forward!

STRONGEST STARTING XI!

Corona
Cruz Azul

Valenzuela
America

Marquez
Leon

Rodriguez
America

Aguilar
America

Guardado
B. Leverkusen

Medina
America

Molina
America

Pena
Leon

J. Hernandez
Man. United

Peralta
Santos Laguna

SUPER SUBS: Munoz, Talavera, Salinas, Ayala, E. Hernandez, Layun, Dos Santos, H. Herrera, Montes, Escoboza, Jimenez, De Nigris.

MEXICO'S HEROES!

PENALTY KING
Javier Hernandez

SPEED MACHINE
Andres Guardado

MUSCLEMAN
Francisco Rodriguez

WONDERKID
Raul Jimenez

MATCH VERDICT!

Mexico went through four coaches in 2013 as their star players went missing in big matches. New coach Herrera will make them hard to beat, but it would be a big shock if they escaped this group!

CAMEROON

| COACH | VOLKER FINKE | WORLD RANKING | 50TH | WORLD CUP ODDS | 400/1 | WORLD CUP BEST | QUARTER-FINALS 1990 |

QUALIFYING FORM!

Cameroon have looked so strong! They totally outclassed Libya, Togo and Congo DR in African Group I to qualify for the play-offs, before destroying Tunisia 4-1 over two legs to book their place in Brazil!

STAR MAN! Alex Song

STRENGTH!

Cameroon's midfield is well tough, and in Samuel Eto'o they still have a quality penalty-box predator!

WEAKNESS!

Eto'o is treated like a king! His influence on tactics and player selection can affect team spirit!

STRONGEST STARTING XI!

Itandje
Konyaspor

N'Koulou
Marseille

Mbia
Sevilla

Chedjou
Galatasaray

Bedimo
Lyon

Makoun
Rennes

Song
Barcelona

Enoh
Antalyaspor

Moukandjo
Nancy

Eto'o
Chelsea

Webo
Fenerbahce

SUPER SUBS: Kameni, N'Dy Assembe, Nounkeu, Matip, Assou-Ekotto, Bong, N'Guemo, Mandjeck, Olinga, N'Djeng, Choupo-Moting, Kweuke.

CAMEROON'S HEROES!

PENALTY KING
Samuel Eto'o

SPEED MACHINE
Benjamin Moukandjo

MUSCLEMAN
Stephane Mbia

WONDERKID
Fabrice Olinga

MATCH VERDICT!

Cameroon are on the verge of becoming a top team, but this World Cup may come too early for their young players. The Indomitable Lions should challenge Croatia for second spot, but will fall just short!

SPAIN

COACH	VICENTE DEL BOSQUE	CAPTAIN	IKER CASILLAS	MOST CAPS	IKER CASILLAS 152

QUALIFYING FORM!

None of the top-seeded teams in the European qualifiers wanted to draw France from Pot 2, but that's exactly what happened to Spain! Vicente del Bosque's team drew with them in Madrid, but then beat them in the return match in Paris and won away in Georgia, Belarus and Finland to top the group!

THE TACTICS!

Spain will probably stick with the 4-2-3-1 formation that helped them win the last World Cup, but they also tested 4-3-3 a few times in qualifying! They could use Cesc Fabregas as a false No.9, or choose to play an out-and-out striker in Diego Costa or Alvaro Negredo!

Cesc Fabregas

STRENGTH!

It's simple – the reigning world and European champions know how to win big football matches! They won all four knockout games 1-0 at the last World Cup. They are machines!

WEAKNESS!

Legendary superstars like Iker Casillas and Xavi are getting on a bit, and Spain sometimes struggle against more aggressive teams!

STAR MAN!

ANDRES INIESTA
BARCELONA

CAPS: 94 GOALS: 11

Iniesta's the most famous player in Spanish footy history after scoring the winning goal in La Roja's 1-0 win against Holland in the 2010 World Cup Final! Four years later and he's hungry for more glory! He's got the class, dribbling skills and experience to shine again!

| MOST GOALS | DAVID VILLA 56 | WORLD RANKING | 1ST | WORLD CUP ODDS | 7/1 | WORLD CUP BEST | WINNERS 2010 |

WATCH OUT FOR...

DIEGO COSTA
ATLETICO MADRID

CAPS: 0 **GOALS:** 0

The Brazil-born striker only agreed to play for Spain this year, and MATCH can't wait to see him in action with La Roja! The powerful Atletico star punishes defences with his strength and finishing!

LAST FIVE RESULTS!

Sep. 10 2013	Spain	2-2	Chile
	Soldado 38, Navas 90		Vargas 5, 44
Oct. 11 2013	Spain	2-1	Belarus
	Xavi 61, Negredo 78		Kornilenko 89
Oct. 15 2013	Spain	2-0	Georgia
	Negredo 26, Mata 61		
Nov. 16 2013	E. Guinea	1-2	Spain
	Bermudez 36		Cazorla 13, Juanfran 43
Nov. 19 2013	South Africa	1-0	Spain
	Parker 56		

STRONGEST STARTING XI!

Casillas Real Madrid

Arbeloa Real Madrid
Pique Barcelona
Ramos Real Madrid
Alba Barcelona

Busquets Barcelona
Xavi Barcelona

Pedro Barcelona
Iniesta Barcelona
Silva Man. City

Fabregas Barcelona

SUPER SUBS: Valdes, Reina, Juanfran, Albiol, Monreal, Koke, Alonso, Mata, Navas, Villa, Costa, Negredo.

SPAIN'S HEROES!

PENALTY KING Xavi

SPEED MACHINE Jesus Navas

MUSCLEMAN Sergio Ramos

WONDERKID Koke

MATCH VERDICT!

Spain will go down in history after winning three major international tournaments in a row, and we think they're going to make it four this summer! Their strength in depth is just unbelievable!

HOLLAND

COACH	LOUIS VAN GAAL	WORLD RANKING	9TH	WORLD CUP ODDS	20/1	WORLD CUP BEST	RUNNERS-UP 1974, 1978 & 2010

QUALIFYING FORM!

Holland were totally unstoppable in European qualifying - they twice put four goals past Romania and stuffed Hungary 8-1 as they racked up 34 goals! They were the first European team to seal qualification to Brazil and won Group D in style with nine wins, one draw and no defeats!

Arjen Robben

STRENGTH!

Robin van Persie and Arjen Robben are two of the best attacking players in world footy right now!

WEAKNESS!

Holland's defence looks shakier than a bowl of jelly and lacks top stars - big teams could hurt them!

STAR MAN!

ROBIN VAN PERSIE
Man. United

CAPS: 81 **GOALS:** 41

RVP has been on fire for Holland - the Man. United striker scored the most goals in European World Cup qualifying with 11 strikes! Dutch fans will be desperate to see him bust the net with his lethal left foot tons more times this summer!

LAST FIVE RESULTS!

Sep. 10 2013	Andorra	0-2	Holland Van Persie 50, 54
Oct. 11 2013	Holland Van Persie 16, 44, 53, Strootman 25, Lens 38, Devecseri 65 (og), Van der Vaart 86, Robben 90	8-1	Hungary Dzsudzsak 47 (pen)
Oct. 15 2013	Turkey	0-2	Holland Robben 8, Sneijder 47
Nov. 16 2013	Japan Osako 44, Honda 60	2-2	Holland Van der Vaart 12, Robben 38
Nov. 19 2013	Holland	0-0	Colombia

STRONGEST STARTING XI!

Cillessen
Ajax

Janmaat
Feyenoord

De Vrij
Feyenoord

Martins Indi
Feyenoord

Willems
PSV

Strootman
Roma

Blind
Feyenoord

Robben
Bayern Munich

Sneijder
Galatasaray

Lens
Dynamo Kiev

Van Persie
Man. United

SUPER SUBS: Stekelenburg, Krul, Van der Wiel, Bruma, Vlaar, Fer, Clasie, Schaars, Van der Vaart, Afellay, Kuyt, Huntelaar.

HOLLAND'S HEROES!

PENALTY KING
Robin van Persie

SPEED MACHINE
Arjen Robben

MUSCLEMAN
Ron Vlaar

WONDERKID
Bruno Martins Indi

MATCH VERDICT!

Holland were awesome at the last World Cup, but four years on they look much weaker! They would qualify from most groups, but the quality of Group B could see The Oranje head home early!

brazuca • spain
brazuca • netherlands
brazuca • chile
brazuca • australia

CHILE

| COACH | JORGE SAMPAOLI | WORLD RANKING | 15TH | WORLD CUP ODDS | 50/1 | WORLD CUP BEST | THIRD PLACE 1962 |

QUALIFYING FORM!

Chile finished third in South American qualifying, four points behind winners Argentina! Eduardo Vargas and Arturo Vidal bagged five goals each, while Barcelona's Alexis Sanchez looked in awesome form!

STAR MAN! Alexis Sanchez

STRENGTH!

Their slick passing style destroys teams, and Vidal is one of the world's best midfielders right now!

WEAKNESS!

Chile let in 25 goals in qualifying! Venezuela conceded less than that and they didn't even reach Brazil!

STRONGEST STARTING XI!

Bravo — Real Sociedad
Medel — Cardiff
M. Gonzalez — Flamengo
Jara — Nott'm Forest
Isla — Juventus
Vidal — Juventus
Diaz — Basel
Mena — Santos
Valdivia — Palmeiras
Sanchez — Barcelona
Vargas — Valencia

SUPER SUBS: Herrera, Toselli, Rojas, O. Gonzalez, Carmona, Silva, Aranguiz, Gutierrez, Fernandez, Beausejour, Suazo, Pinilla.

CHILE'S HEROES!

PENALTY KING — Arturo Vidal
SPEED MACHINE — Eduardo Vargas
MUSCLEMAN — Gary Medel
WONDERKID — Felipe Gutierrez

MATCH VERDICT!

Chile have all the ingredients to do really well this summer! We reckon they'll pip Holland to second place behind Spain in Group B, but hosts Brazil will have too much class for them in the last 16!

AUSTRALIA

| COACH | ANGE POSTECOGLOU | WORLD RANKING | 56TH | WORLD CUP ODDS | 1,000/1 | WORLD CUP BEST | LAST 16 2006 |

QUALIFYING FORM!

Australia bagged a bye to the third round of Asian qualifying and won Group D with 15 points! The fourth round saw The Socceroos qualify from Group B in second place, four points behind winners Japan!

STAR MAN! Tim Cahill

STRENGTH!

Crystal Palace star Mile Jedinak has vital Prem experience and Tim Cahill is a legendary finisher!

WEAKNESS!

All their best players are over 30 and slower than your gran! They'll find breaking down defences tough!

STRONGEST STARTING XI!

Galekovic — Adelaide United
Wilkshire — Dynamo Moscow
Neill — Unattached
Ognenovski — Umm-Salal
McKay — Brisbane Roar
Jedinak — Crystal Palace
Milligan — Melbourne V.
Kruse — B. Leverkusen
Holman — Al-Nasr
Oar — Utrecht
Cahill — NY Red Bulls

SUPER SUBS: Ryan, Langerak, Franjic, North, McGowan, Thwaite, Valeri, Rogic, Bresciano, Vidosic, Thompson, Kennedy.

AUSTRALIA'S HEROES!

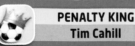
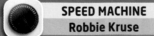
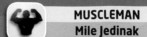
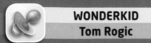

PENALTY KING — Tim Cahill
SPEED MACHINE — Robbie Kruse
MUSCLEMAN — Mile Jedinak
WONDERKID — Tom Rogic

MATCH VERDICT!

Australians have been crying about the World Cup draw since December! Cahill has to play as a false No.9 because they've got no strikers and their stars are getting old! They're going home early!

BIG '10

It's time to test your footy brain with these rock-hard questions on the teams in Groups A and B!

1 Brazil have won the World Cup five times, but how many times have they finished as runners-up?

2 Which animal features in the nickname of Cameroon's national football team?

3 Which MLS club does Australia midfielder Tim Cahill play for?

4 How much did Cardiff pay to sign Chile's Gary Medel last summer – £8 million or £11 million?

5 Which Prem team did Brazil's Luiz Felipe Scolari manage between 2008 and 2009?

6 Which Bayern Munich star will miss Croatia's first match of the World Cup after being sent off against Iceland in the play-offs?

7 True or False? Holland were the first European team to qualify for this summer's World Cup!

8 Name this rapid PSG and Holland defender!

9 How old is awesome Spain striker David Villa – 30, 32 or 34 years old?

10 Seven Barcelona players started for Spain in the 2010 World Cup Final, but which was the youngest?

ANSWERS ON PAGE 90

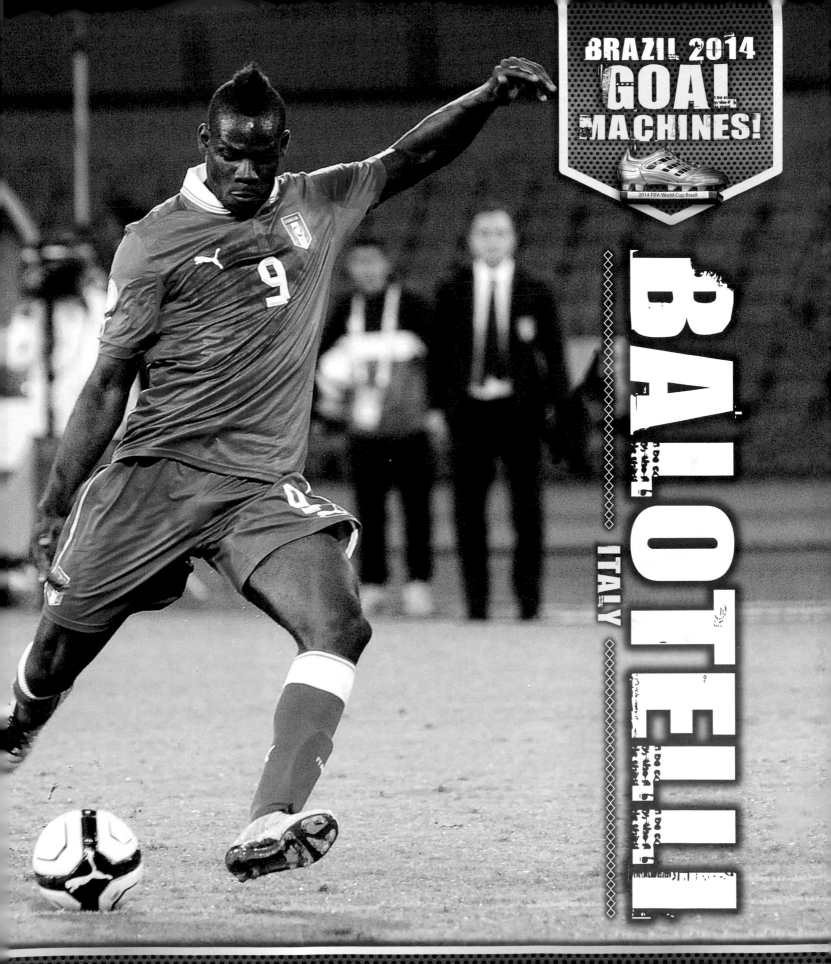

BALOTELLI

ITALY

Mario netted every one of his 21 penalties in official matches before missing his first ever spot-kick against Napoli last September!

Balo was Italy's top scorer in World Cup qualifying! The ex-Man. City striker bagged five goals in just five games for The Azzurri!

Balotelli's won the Champions League, Prem, three Serie A titles, FA Cup, Coppa Italia, Italian Supercup and Community Shield during his career!

COLOMBIA

COACH	JOSE PEKERMAN	CAPTAIN	MARIO YEPES	MOST CAPS	MARIO YEPES 94

QUALIFYING FORM!

Colombia finished two points behind table-toppers Argentina in South America's massive qualifying group to book their place in Brazil! Los Cafeteros thrashed Uruguay, Chile and Bolivia along the way with Radamel Falcao bagging nine goals! But their high point came when they bossed Argentina's deadly attack in a 0-0 draw in Buenos Aires!

THE TACTICS!

Ancient boss Jose Pekerman prefers 4-4-2, but might switch to 4-2-3-1 if Falcao misses out! Pacy full-backs Juan Zuniga and Pablo Armero love to bomb forward, while the wingers are given a free role to make things happen in the final third!

Pablo Armero

STRENGTH!

Colombia love hot conditions, so expect their lethal attack and tactical genius of a coach to turn the weather to their advantage!

WEAKNESS!

Their World Cup record is absolutely shocking! They've made it to the knockout stages just once in their history, and they usually flop when the pressure's on to perform!

STAR MAN!

JAMES RODRIGUEZ
MONACO

Caps: 20 **Goals:** 3

Rodriguez will be one of the most exciting players to watch at Brazil 2014! His movement, touch and vision ties defenders in knots, and his understanding with team-mate at club level Falcao is unbelievable! If El Tigre is fit for Brazil, his link-up play with J-Rod will blow your mind!

WATCH OUT FOR...

RADAMEL FALCAO
MONACO

Caps: 51 **Goals:** 20

Colombia's main man was ruled out of the World Cup with a knee injury back in January, but when it comes to Falcao, anything's possible! The lethal striker heals faster than he runs, so could still make it!

LAST FIVE RESULTS!

Sep. 10 2013	Uruguay	2-0	Colombia
	Cavani 77, Stuani 81		
Oct. 11 2013	Colombia	3-3	Chile
	Gutierrez 69, Falcao 75, 84 (pens)		Vidal 19 (pen), Sanchez 22, 29
Oct. 15 2013	Paraguay	1-2	Colombia
	Rojas 8		Yepes 38, 57
Nov. 14 2013	Belgium	0-2	Colombia
			Falcao 51, Ibarbo 66
Nov. 19 2013	Holland	0-0	Colombia

STRONGEST STARTING XI!

Ospina Nice

Zuniga Napoli — **Perea** Cruz Azul — **Zapata** AC Milan — **Armero** West Ham

Sanchez Elche — **Aguilar** Toulouse

Cuadrado Fiorentina — **Gutierrez** River Plate — **Rodriguez** Monaco

Martinez Porto

SUPER SUBS: Mondragon, Vargas, Medina, Arias, Valdes, Yepes, Torres, Guarin, Ramirez, Bacca, Ramos, Falcao.

COLOMBIA'S HEROES!

PENALTY KING Radamel Falcao

SPEED MACHINE Juan G. Cuadrado

MUSCLEMAN Carlos Sanchez

WONDERKID James Rodriguez

MATCH VERDICT!

If Colombia are anywhere near their best, they'll batter Greece, Japan and Ivory Coast to win Group C! But, and this is massive, if Falcao isn't fit by the time it's the last 16, England will send them home!

IVORY COAST

| COACH | SABRI LAMOUCHI | WORLD RANKING | 17TH | WORLD CUP ODDS | 100/1 | WORLD CUP BEST | GROUP STAGE 2006 & 2010 |

QUALIFYING FORM!

Ivory Coast cruised through Group C in Africa with Lacina Traore, Wilfried Bony and the Toure brothers among the goals! Senegal were a tougher test in the play-offs, but Salomon Kalou's goal sealed a 4-2 aggregate win and World Cup qualification!

Didier Drogba

STRENGTH!

They have some of the strongest, fastest and most skilful African attackers in history to choose from! They won't struggle for goals!

WEAKNESS!

The Elephants' defence loses focus at crucial moments, and Boubacar Barry lets in too many soft goals!

LAST FIVE RESULTS!

Jun. 8 2013	Gambia	0-3	Ivory Coast
			Traore 12, Bony 61, Y. Toure 89
Jun. 16 2013	Tanzania	2-4	Ivory Coast
	Kiemba 2, Ulimwengu 34		Traore 13, Y. Toure 23, 43 (pen), Bony 90
Sep. 7 2013	Ivory Coast	1-1	Morocco
	Drogba 83 (pen)		El Arabi 52
Oct. 12 2013	Ivory Coast	3-1	Senegal
	Drogba 5 (pen), Sane 14 (og), Kalou 49		Cisse 90
Nov. 16 2013	Senegal	1-1	Ivory Coast
	Sow 72 (pen)		Kalou 90

STAR MAN!

YAYA TOURE

MAN. CITY

Caps: 82 **Goals:** 16

Toure has the power and pace to steam-roll opponents out of matches, and that's exactly what he's been doing all season! He's also perfected his dipping free-kicks, so get ready for Yaya to become a true World Cup star in Brazil!

STRONGEST STARTING XI!

Barry — Lokeren

Aurier — Toulouse

K. Toure — Liverpool

Zokora — Trabzonspor

Boka — Stuttgart

Tiote — Newcastle

Romaric — Bastia

Gervinho — Roma

Y. Toure — Man. City

Kalou — Lille

Drogba — Galatasaray

SUPER SUBS: Gbohouo, Karim Cisse, Bamba, Angoua, Tiene, Gosso, Bolly, Akpa-Akpro, Sio, Kone, Traore, Bony.

IVORY COAST'S HEROES!

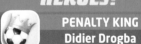

PENALTY KING Didier Drogba

SPEED MACHINE Mathis Bolly

MUSCLEMAN Yaya Toure

WONDERKID Serge Aurier

MATCH VERDICT!

Ivory Coast have never made it past the World Cup group stage! But with top attacking players and opponents with major weaknesses to punish, they should definitely make it into round two this time!

JAPAN

COACH	ALBERTO ZACCHERONI	WORLD RANKING	48TH	WORLD CUP ODDS	125/1	WORLD CUP BEST	LAST 16 2002 & 2010

QUALIFYING FORM!

Japan became the first team to qualify for Brazil 2014 when Keisuke Honda buried an injury-time penalty to snatch a draw against Australia! They finished top of Asian Group B with five wins from eight matches!

STAR MAN! Keisuke Honda

STRENGTH!

Samurai Blue have great attacking midfielders and a defence that only conceded five goals in qualifying!

WEAKNESS!

Their team is filled with bench-warmers and J-League stars! The step-up in class might be too much!

STRONGEST STARTING XI!

Kawashima
Standard Liege

Uchida
Schalke

Konno
Gamba Osaka

Yoshida
Southampton

Nagatomo
Inter Milan

Endo
Gamba Osaka

Hasebe
Nuremberg

Okazaki
Mainz

Honda
AC Milan

Kagawa
Man. United

Kakitani
Cerezo Osaka

SUPER SUBS: Nishikawa, Gonda, G. Sakai, Morishige, Inoha, H. Sakai, Hosogai, Takahashi, Yamaguchi, Inui, Kiyotake, Osako.

JAPAN'S HEROES!

PENALTY KING
Keisuke Honda

SPEED MACHINE
Yuto Nagatomo

MUSCLEMAN
Masahiko Inoha

WONDERKID
Gotoku Sakai

MATCH VERDICT!

Japan proved in the qualifiers that their attack and defence is probably the best in Asia! But Colombia's creative kings and the power of Ivory Coast should mean Samurai Blue just miss out on second spot!

GREECE

COACH	FERNANDO SANTOS	WORLD RANKING	12TH	WORLD CUP ODDS	200/1	WORLD CUP BEST	GROUP STAGES 1994 & 2010

QUALIFYING FORM!

Greece ground out loads of tight wins to finish second in European Group G. They faced Romania in the play-offs, but four class goals from Kostas Mitroglou and Dimitris Salpingidis sent them through!

STAR MAN! Kostas Mitroglou

STRENGTH!

Greece aren't exciting, but they're incredibly tough to beat! They only conceded four goals in Group G!

WEAKNESS!

Gaffer Santos has an ageing squad to pick from and many of his stars aren't as good as they used to be!

STRONGEST STARTING XI!

Karnezis
Granada

Torosidis
Roma

Papastathopoulos
Borussia Dortmund

Siovas
Olympiakos

Holebas
Olympiakos

Maniatis
Olympiakos

Tziolis
Kayserispor

Katsouranis
PAOK

Salpingidis
PAOK

Samaras
Celtic

Mitroglou
Fulham

SUPER SUBS: Sifakis, Kapino, Vyntra, Manolas, Tzavelas, Samaris, Kone, Karagounis, Ninis, Christodoulopoulos, Fortounis, Gekas.

GREECE'S HEROES!

PENALTY KING
Giorgos Karagounis

SPEED MACHINE
Dimitris Salpingidis

MUSCLEMAN
Kostas Mitroglou

WONDERKID
Stefanos Kapino

MATCH VERDICT!

Greece can't be ignored – their defence is solid and their strikers are dangerous – but their lack of midfield quality and ageing stars mean they're most likely to finish bottom of Group C!

ENGLAND

| COACH | ROY HODGSON | CAPTAIN | STEVEN GERRARD | MOST CAPS | STEVEN GERRARD 108 |

2014 FIFA World Cup Brazil™ Qualifiers
ENGLAND

QUALIFYING FORM!

England finished unbeaten in their qualifying group, but they still had to wait until the final game to seal their place in Brazil. The Three Lions only bagged wins against minnows Moldova and San Marino going into their final two qualifiers, but epic victories against Montenegro and Poland at Wembley saw them edge out Ukraine for top spot!

THE TACTICS!

England play a 4-2-3-1 system with Wayne Rooney at the heart of everything good they do! Andros Townsend and Leighton Baines provide the width, while Steven Gerrard and Jack Wilshere control the midfield with their awesome range of passing!

Andros Townsend

STRENGTH!

The Three Lions are famous for their incredible passion, and they try to play games at a high tempo to overwhelm their opponents!

WEAKNESS!

England can sometimes play too many long balls, and often struggle to keep possession against the bigger footballing nations!

STAR MAN!

WAYNE ROONEY
MAN. UNITED

CAPS: 88 **GOALS:** 38

Wazza's powerful, has great vision, packs a rocket shot and is a big-game player – 28 of his 38 England goals have come in competitive matches! He struggled with injury and form in 2006 and 2010, but now he's ready to make his mark on football's most famous tournament in Brazil!

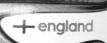

| MOST GOALS | WAYNE ROONEY 38 | WORLD RANKING | 13TH | WORLD CUP ODDS | 25/1 | WORLD CUP BEST | WINNERS 1966 |

WATCH OUT FOR....

JACK WILSHERE
ARSENAL

CAPS: 14 **GOALS:** 0

Wilshere made his England debut nearly four years ago, but he's finally shaken off his injury problems and is ready to cement his place in midfield. He dominates opponents with his technique and passing!

LAST FIVE RESULTS!

| Sep. 10 2013 | Ukraine | 0-0 | England |
| Oct. 11 2013 | England | 4-1 | Montenegro |

Rooney 49, Boskovic 62 (og), Townsend 78, Sturridge 90 — Damjanovic 71

| Oct. 15 2013 | England | 2-0 | Poland |

Rooney 41, Gerrard 88

| Nov. 15 2013 | England | 0-2 | Chile |

Sanchez 7, 90

| Nov. 19 2013 | England | 0-1 | Germany |

Mertesacker 39

STRONGEST STARTING XI!

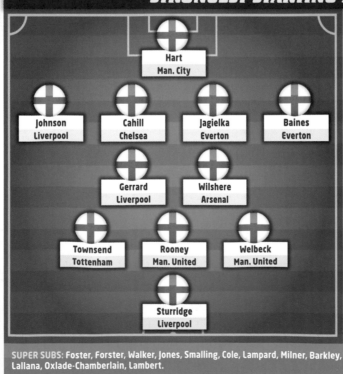

Hart — Man. City

Johnson Liverpool — **Cahill** Chelsea — **Jagielka** Everton — **Baines** Everton

Gerrard Liverpool — **Wilshere** Arsenal

Townsend Tottenham — **Rooney** Man. United — **Welbeck** Man. United

Sturridge Liverpool

SUPER SUBS: Foster, Forster, Walker, Jones, Smalling, Cole, Lampard, Milner, Barkley, Lallana, Oxlade-Chamberlain, Lambert.

ENGLAND'S HEROES!

PENALTY KING
Steven Gerrard

SPEED MACHINE
Kyle Walker

MUSCLEMAN
Wayne Rooney

WONDERKID
Ross Barkley

MATCH VERDICT!

We reckon The Three Lions have enough quality to make it out of the group of death, but a potential quarter-final showdown with host nation Brazil could be a step too far for Roy Hodgson's side!

URUGUAY

COACH	OSCAR TABAREZ	WORLD RANKING	6TH	WORLD CUP ODDS	20/1	WORLD CUP BEST	WINNERS 1930 & 1950

QUALIFYING FORM!

Uruguay are a lot of experts' dark horses to win the tournament, but they only just qualified for this summer's finals! They struggled in the South American qualifying section to finish fifth, but battered Jordan 5-0 in the World Cup play-offs to book their spot in Brazil!

Edinson Cavani

STRENGTH!

They've got one of the most lethal strikeforces at the tournament, plus Diego Forlan warms the bench!

WEAKNESS!

Uruguay are famous for being one of the toughest nations in world footy, but they often lose their discipline!

LAST FIVE RESULTS!

Sep. 10 2013	Uruguay	2-0	Colombia
	Cavani 77, Stuani 80		
Oct. 11 2013	Ecuador	1-0	Uruguay
	Montero 30		
Oct. 15 2013	Uruguay	3-2	Argentina
	C. Rodriguez 6, Suarez 34 (pen), Cavani 49		M. Rodriguez 14, 41
Nov. 13 2013	Jordan	0-5	Uruguay
			M. Pereira 22, Stuani 42, Lodeiro 70, C. Rodriguez 78, Suarez 90
Nov. 20 2013	Uruguay	0-0	Jordan

STAR MAN!

LUIS SUAREZ
LIVERPOOL
CAPS: 76 **GOALS:** 39

Suarez has ripped up the Prem all season and has been doing the same for his country! He was top scorer in qualifying alongside Holland's Robin van Persie and Belize striker Deon McCauley with 11 goals, and links up brilliantly with Edinson Cavani!

STRONGEST STARTING XI!

Muslera
Galatasaray

M. Pereira
Benfica

Lugano
West Brom

Godin
Atletico Madrid

Caceres
Juventus

Stuani
Espanyol

Perez
Bologna

Arevalo
Morelia

Rodriguez
Atletico Madrid

Cavani
PSG

Suarez
Liverpool

SUPER SUBS: Silva, Castillo, Fucile, Scotti, Gimenez, Gargano, A. Pereira, Gonzalez, Ramirez, Lodeiro, Forlan, Hernandez.

URUGUAY'S HEROES!

PENALTY KING
Luis Suarez

SPEED MACHINE
Abel Hernandez

MUSCLEMAN
Edinson Cavani

WONDERKID
Jose Maria Gimenez

MATCH VERDICT!

The climate will suit Uruguay, they won the World Cup when it was last hosted in Brazil in 1950 and Suarez is in the form of his life! We're backing them to get to the quarter-finals at least!

ITALY

COACH	CESARE PRANDELLI	WORLD RANKING	7TH	WORLD CUP ODDS	18/1	WORLD CUP BEST	WINNERS 1934, 1938, 1982 & 2006

QUALIFYING FORM!

The Azzurri cruised through their group ahead of Denmark, Czech Republic and Bulgaria with two games to spare! They're one of just seven European teams to finish the qualifying campaign unbeaten!

STAR MAN! *Mario Balotelli*

STRENGTH!

Italy are masters at outsmarting their opponents with their tactics and have a rock-solid defence!

WEAKNESS!

Mario Balotelli proved at Euro 2012 that he can destroy teams on the big stage, but he's so inconsistent!

STRONGEST STARTING XI!

Buffon
Juventus

Abate
AC Milan

Barzagli
Juventus

Bonucci
Juventus

Chiellini
Juventus

De Rossi
Roma

Pirlo
Juventus

Marchisio
Juventus

Montolivo
AC Milan

Insigne
Napoli

Balotelli
AC Milan

SUPER SUBS: Sirigu, Marchetti, Maggio, Ranocchia, Criscito, Motta, Verratti, Candreva, Diamanti, El Shaarawy, Osvaldo, Rossi.

ITALY'S HEROES!

PENALTY KING
Mario Balotelli

SPEED MACHINE
Ignazio Abate

MUSCLEMAN
Giorgio Chiellini

WONDERKID
Lorenzo Insigne

MATCH VERDICT!

Italy have a great World Cup record and are famous for their tactics, but they could be heading home after the group stages! We think it's between them and England for the runners-up spot!

COSTA RICA

COACH	JORGE LUIS PINTO	WORLD RANKING	32ND	WORLD CUP ODDS	600/1	WORLD CUP BEST	LAST 16 1990

QUALIFYING FORM!

Los Ticos sailed through to Brazil after finishing second in CONCACAF's final qualifying group. They won all five of their home games and had the best defensive record – they conceded just seven goals!

STAR MAN! *Bryan Ruiz*

STRENGTH!

Bryan Ruiz's playmaking skills and Joel Campbell's lightning pace will cause trouble for most defences!

WEAKNESS!

Bryan Oviedo's absence from the squad with a broken leg hugely weakens their left-hand side!

STRONGEST STARTING XI!

Navas
Levante

Acosta
Alajuelense

Gonzalez
Valerenga

Umana
Saprissa

Gamboa
Rosenborg

Diaz
Mainz

Borges
AIK

Tejeda
Saprissa

Ruiz
PSV

Bolanos
Copenhagen

Campbell
Olympiakos

SUPER SUBS: Pemberton, Moreira, Salvatierra, Meneses, Miller, Cubero, Barrantes, Rodriguez, Calvo, Brenes, Arrieta, Saborio.

COSTA RICA'S HEROES!

PENALTY KING
Alvaro Saborio

SPEED MACHINE
Joel Campbell

MUSCLEMAN
Celso Borges

WONDERKID
Joel Campbell

MATCH VERDICT!

Costa Rica will be the whipping boys in Group D! Arsenal's on-loan striker Joel Campbell will be one to watch, but we don't think they'll have the quality to trouble the big three!

SPOT THE STARS

Find ten superstars in this crowd who are ruled out of World Cup 2014!

1	ZLATAN IBRAHIMOVIC	✓	6	BRANISLAV IVANOVIC	✓
2	GARETH BALE	✓	7	CHRISTIAN ERIKSEN	✓
3	THEO WALCOTT	✓	8	SEAMUS COLEMAN	✓
4	AARON RAMSEY	✓	9	SCOTT BROWN	✓
5	BRYAN OVIEDO	✓	10	JONNY EVANS	✓

ANSWERS ON PAGE 90

VAN PERSIE

HOLLAND

The lethal Dutch striker finished as top scorer in the European section of World Cup 2014 qualification, with 11 goals in just nine games!

The striker has won the Premier League Golden Boot for the last two seasons, hitting 30 in 2011-12 and 26 in 2012-13!

Van Persie is Holland's record goalscorer, having netted 41 goals in just 81 appearances for The Oranje! What a legend!

FRANCE

| COACH | DIDIER DESCHAMPS | CAPTAIN | HUGO LLORIS | MOST CAPS | FRANCK RIBERY 80 |

QUALIFYING FORM!

France should count themselves lucky to be in Brazil! After finishing runners-up to Spain in Group I of Europe's qualifying section, they lost the first leg of their play-off against Ukraine 2-0! But a stunning comeback in Paris saw Les Bleus win 3-0 to seal an amazing win!

THE TACTICS!

France's 4-2-3-1 system suits their players perfectly! Blaise Matuidi's tough-tackling and Paul Pogba's raw power dominate the midfield, Mathieu Debuchy and Patrice Evra's pace provides penetration on the flanks, and the three attacking midfielders create tons of chances for lethal striker Karim Benzema!

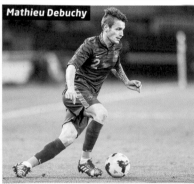

Mathieu Debuchy

STRENGTH!

Les Bleus have tons of individually gifted players – Pogba, Samir Nasri, Yohan Cabaye, Olivier Giroud, Loic Remy, Franck Ribery and Benzema are all potential match winners!

WEAKNESS!

The team are often criticised for not being united, and big fall-outs in their squad have harmed their chances in past tournaments!

STAR MAN!

FRANCK RIBERY
BAYERN MUNICH

CAPS: 80 **GOALS:** 16

The electric winger has everything in his locker to destroy full-backs – lightning pace, tons of tricks, close dribbling skills and massive confidence! He's won everything with his club during the last year, and now he's hoping to fire his country to glory this summer!

WATCH OUT FOR...

PAUL POGBA
JUVENTUS

CAPS: 7 **GOALS:** 3

The ex-Man. United wonderkid is one of the most explosive midfielders on the planet! His box-to-box runs are legendary, he's got mega-quick feet and he scores tons of worldies with his rocket long shots!

LAST FIVE RESULTS!

Sep. 10 2013
Belarus **2-4** France
Filipenko 32, Kalachev 57 — Ribery 47 (pen), 64, Nasri 71, Pogba 73

Oct. 11 2013
France **6-0** Australia
Ribery 8 (pen), Giroud 16, 27, Cabaye 29, Debuchy 47, Benzema 51

Oct. 15 2013
France **3-0** Poland
Ribery 8, Toivio 76 (og), Benzema 87

Nov. 15 2013
Ukraine **2-0** France
Zozulya 62, Yarmolenko 82 (pen)

Nov. 19 2013
France **3-0** Ukraine
Sakho 22, 72, Benzema 34

STRONGEST STARTING XI!

Lloris — Tottenham

Debuchy — Newcastle
Koscielny — Arsenal
Sakho — Liverpool
Evra — Man. United

Matuidi — PSG
Pogba — Juventus

Valbuena — Marseille
Cabaye — PSG
Ribery — Bayern Munich

Benzema — Real Madrid

SUPER SUBS: Mandanda, Landreau, Sagna, Varane, Abidal, Clichy, Mavuba, Sissoko, Grenier, Nasri, Remy, Giroud.

FRANCE'S HEROES!

PENALTY KING
Franck Ribery

SPEED MACHINE
Franck Ribery

MUSCLEMAN
Paul Pogba

WONDERKID
Raphael Varane

MATCH VERDICT!

France have the potential to be real contenders, but we're predicting an early exit for them! They finished bottom of their group in two of the last three World Cups, and we think they'll flop again!

SWITZERLAND

| COACH | OTTMAR HITZFELD | WORLD RANKING | 8TH | WORLD CUP ODDS | 66/1 | WORLD CUP BEST | QUARTER-FINALS 1934, 1938 & 1954 |

QUALIFYING FORM!

Switzerland had one of the easiest European qualifying groups and sealed their place in Brazil with a game to spare! They won seven and drew three to finish the campaign unbeaten, and conceded just six goals in ten games - four of which came in the 4-4 draw with Iceland!

Valon Behrami

STRENGTH!

The Swiss play as a team and not as individuals, so they often shock the more talented nations!

WEAKNESS!

Switzerland lack a top-class striker. They hit 17 goals in qualifying, and just three were scored by strikers!

LAST FIVE RESULTS!

Sep. 6 2013	**Switzerland** Lichtsteiner 15, 30, Schar 27, Dzemaili 54 (pen)	4-4	**Iceland** Gudmundsson 3, 68, 90, Sigthorsson 56
Sep. 10 2013	**Norway**	0-2	**Switzerland** Schar 12, 51
Oct. 11 2013	**Albania** Salihi 89 (pen)	1-2	**Switzerland** Shaqiri 47, Lang 77
Oct. 15 2013	**Switzerland** Xhaka 74	1-0	**Slovenia**
Nov. 15 2013	**South Korea** Jeong-Ho Hong 59 Chung-Yong Lee 87	2-1	**Switzerland** Kasami 7

STAR MAN!

XHERDAN SHAQIRI
BAYERN MUNICH

CAPS: 30 **GOALS:** 8

Shaqiri doesn't start often for his club, but he's one of the first names on the team sheet for his country! The tiny winger is quick, a tricky dribbler, tough to knock off the ball and has a wand of a left foot - he's Switzerland's main match-winner!

STRONGEST STARTING XI!

Benaglio
Wolfsburg

Lichtsteiner
Juventus

Schar
Basel

Von Bergen
Young Boys

Rodriguez
Wolfsburg

Behrami
Napoli

Inler
Napoli

Shaqiri
Bayern Munich

Xhaka
B. M'gladbach

Stocker
Basel

Seferovic
Real Sociedad

SUPER SUBS: Sommer, Wolfli, Djourou, Senderos, Ziegler, Dzemaili, Fernandes, Kasami, Barnetta, Mehmedi, Gavranovic, Derdiyok.

SWITZERLAND'S HEROES!

PENALTY KING
Gokhan Inler

SPEED MACHINE
Xherdan Shaqiri

MUSCLEMAN
Gokhan Inler

WONDERKID
Granit Xhaka

MATCH VERDICT!

The Swiss aren't top seeds for nothing - they just don't lose competitive games very often! We're backing them to qualify from Group E, but Argentina will be too good for them in the last 16!

ECUADOR

COACH	REINALDO RUEDA	WORLD RANKING	23RD	WORLD CUP ODDS	125/1	WORLD CUP BEST	LAST 16 2006

QUALIFYING FORM!

Ecuador were second in the South American group after ten games, thanks to an epic home record! But they then won just one of their last six games, against Uruguay, to claim the last automatic qualification spot!

STAR MAN! Jefferson Montero

STRENGTH!

Ecuador have some top attacking players and love to cause teams problems with their pace and skill!

WEAKNESS!

They might be great going forward, but Ecuador aren't brilliant at the back and concede lots of goals!

STRONGEST STARTING XI!

Dominguez — LDU Quito

Paredes — Barcelona (Ecu)
Guagua — Emelec
Erazo — Flamengo
W. Ayovi — Pachuca

A. Valencia — Man. United
Castillo — Al-Hilal
Noboa — Dynamo Moscow
Montero — Morelia

Caicedo — Al-Jazira
E. Valencia — Pachuca

SUPER SUBS: Banguera, Bone, Achilier, Campos, Bagui, Ramirez, Saritama, Rojas, Ibarra, Martinez, Gaibor, J. Ayovi.

ECUADOR'S HEROES!

PENALTY KING
Felipe Caicedo

SPEED MACHINE
Joao Rojas

MUSCLEMAN
Felipe Caicedo

WONDERKID
Cristian Ramirez

MATCH VERDICT!

This might be controversial, but we reckon Ecuador will win Group E! They've got top attacking talent in their team and are used to the conditions, and that could be enough to grab top spot!

HONDURAS

COACH	LUIS FERNANDO SUAREZ	WORLD RANKING	43RD	WORLD CUP ODDS	1,500/1	WORLD CUP BEST	GROUP STAGES 1982 & 2010

QUALIFYING FORM!

Honduras bagged the last of the automatic qualification spots in the CONCACAF group with a 2-2 draw in their final game against Jamaica. It means they've qualified for the last two World Cups on the trot!

STAR MAN! Carlos Costly

STRENGTH!

The Hondurans will be used to the hot and sticky conditions in Brazil more than most teams at the finals!

WEAKNESS!

They're just not very good! Even their best stars will find it tough against the world's best players!

STRONGEST STARTING XI!

Valladares — Olimpia

Beckeles — Olimpia
Bernardez — San Jose E.
Figueroa — Hull
Izaguirre — Celtic

O.B. Garcia — Houston Dynamo
Garrido — Olimpia
Palacios — Stoke
Espinoza — Wigan

Costly — Real Espana
Bengtson — New England R.

SUPER SUBS: Bodden, Escobar, Peralta, J.C. Garcia, Montes, Claros, Chavez, Alvarez, Delgado, Najar, J. Palacios, Martinez.

HONDURAS' HEROES!

PENALTY KING
Carlos Costly

SPEED MACHINE
Marvin Chavez

MUSCLEMAN
Victor Bernardez

WONDERKID
Andy Najar

MATCH VERDICT!

They'll be more suited to the conditions than most in Brazil and will give it everything they've got, but MATCH will be amazed if Honduras make it to the knockout stages. An early exit looks certain!

ARGENTINA

COACH	ALEJANDRO SABELLA	CAPTAIN	LIONEL MESSI	MOST CAPS	JAVIER MASCHERANO 95

QUALIFYING FORM!

The South American section of World Cup qualifying is the most competitive on the planet, but Argentina sailed through the group in first place with nine wins and five draws from their 16 games! They did the double over Chile – smashing them 4-1 at home – won away in Colombia, stuffed Uruguay 3-0 and hammered Ecuador 4-0! Lionel Messi bagged ten goals and Gonzalo Higuain netted nine!

THE TACTICS!

Argentina gaffer Alejandro Sabella plays a 4-3-3 formation in most games, with Messi used in a free role between midfield and attack! He switched to 5-3-2 for tough away games in qualifying, so they will be ready for every opponent!

Javier Mascherano

STRENGTH!

Argentina have the best attacking talent in the tournament! Messi + Tevez + Higuain + Aguero = GOALS!

WEAKNESS!

Sabella's side only conceded 15 goals in 16 qualifying games, but we still think their defence will struggle against big teams!

STAR MAN!
LIONEL MESSI
BARCELONA

CAPS: 83 **GOALS:** 37

Leo is arguably the greatest footy star of all time, and is desperate to bring his A-game to Brazil after failing to score a goal at the 2010 World Cup! He was the second top scorer in South American qualifying behind Luis Suarez, and defenders have nightmares about him!

WATCH OUT FOR....

SERGIO AGUERO
MAN. CITY

CAPS: 49 **GOALS:** 21

This could be Aguero's time to shine! Messi usually steals the headlines for Argentina, but Kun has been one of the Prem's hottest stars in 2013-14 and he's ready to take his club form to Brazil!

LAST FIVE RESULTS!

Sep. 11 2013	**Paraguay** Nunez 17, Santa Cruz 86	**2-5**	**Argentina** Messi 12 & 53 (pens), Aguero 32, Di Maria 50, M. Rodriguez 90
Oct. 12 2013	**Argentina** Lavezzi 23, 35, Palacio 47	**3-1**	**Peru** Pizarro 21
Oct. 16 2013	**Uruguay** C. Rodriguez 6, Suarez 34 (pen), Cavani 49	**3-2**	**Argentina** M. Rodriguez 14, 41
Nov. 16 2013	**Ecuador**	**0-0**	**Argentina**
Nov. 19 2013	**Argentina** Aguero 40, 66	**2-0**	**Bosnia-Herz.**

STRONGEST STARTING XI!

Romero
Monaco

Zabaleta
Man. City

F. Fernandez
Napoli

Garay
Benfica

Rojo
Sporting Lisbon

Banega
Newell's O.B.

Mascherano
Barcelona

Di Maria
Real Madrid

Aguero
Man. City

Messi
Barcelona

Higuain
Napoli

SUPER SUBS: Andujar, Orion, Peruzzi, Basanta, Campagnaro, Coloccini, Biglia, Gago, M. Rodriguez, Tevez, Lavezzi, Palacio.

ARGENTINA'S HEROES!

PENALTY KING
Lionel Messi

SPEED MACHINE
Angel di Maria

MUSCLEMAN
Ever Banega

WONDERKID
Gino Peruzzi

MATCH VERDICT!

Argentina are used to the South American climate and have one of the greatest players of all time in their attack, so they can definitely go all the way. But we think they'll crash out in the semis!

BOSNIA-HERZ.

| COACH | SAFET SUSIC | WORLD RANKING | 19TH | WORLD CUP ODDS | 200/1 | WORLD CUP BEST | NEVER PLAYED! |

QUALIFYING FORM!

Bosnia & Herzegovina booked their plane tickets to Brazil after winning a dramatic group in Europe's section of the draw. They finished joint-top with Greece in Group G on 25 points, but Safet Susic's team came first on goal difference thanks to massive wins over Liechtenstein and Latvia!

Miralem Pjanic

STRENGTH!

Midfielder Miralem Pjanic has been awesome for Roma this season and Edin Dzeko loves scoring goals!

WEAKNESS!

This is Bosnia & Herzegovina's first World Cup and their lack of big game experience could hurt them

LAST FIVE RESULTS!

Sep. 6 2013	Bosnia-Herz.	0-1	Slovakia Pecovsky 77
Sep. 10 2013	Slovakia Hamsik 42	1-2	Bosnia-Herz. Bicakcic 70, Hajrovic 78
Oct. 11 2013	Bosnia-Herz. Dzeko 27, 39, Misimovic 34, Ibisevic 38	4-1	Liechtenstein Hasler 61
Oct. 15 2013	Lithuania	0-1	Bosnia-Herz. Ibisevic 68
Nov. 19 2013	Argentina Aguero 40, 66	2-0	Bosnia-Herz.

STAR MAN!

EDIN DZEKO
MAN. CITY
CAPS: 59 **GOALS:** 33

The Man. City star was the second top scorer in European qualification behind RVP with ten goals! Dzeko's in and out of City's team, but he's the main man for his country! His headers and finishing skills could make him a Golden Boot contender!

STRONGEST STARTING XI!

Begovic — Stoke

Vrsajevic — Hajduk Split
Bicakcic — E. Braunschweig
Spahic — B. Leverkusen
Salihovic — Hoffenheim

Pjanic — Roma
Medunjanin — Gaziantepspor
Misimovic — Guizhou Renhe
Lulic — Lazio

Ibisevic — Stuttgart
Dzeko — Man. City

SUPER SUBS: Fejzic, Avdukic, Mujdza, Sunjic, Kolasinac, Zahirovic, Visca, Ibricic, Kvrzic, Rahimic, Stevanovic, Hajrovic.

BOSNIA'S HEROES!

PENALTY KING
Edin Dzeko

SPEED MACHINE
Senad Lulic

MUSCLEMAN
Emir Spahic

WONDERKID
Sead Kolasinac

MATCH VERDICT!

Bosnia & Herzegovina might be new to the World Cup, but they've got a great chance of getting out of the group! The likes of Pjanic, Dzeko and Ibisevic could easily fire them to the quarter-finals!

IRAN

| COACH | CARLOS QUEIROZ | WORLD RANKING | 34TH | WORLD CUP ODDS | 1,500/1 | WORLD CUP BEST | GROUP STAGE 1978, 1998 & 2006 |

QUALIFYING FORM!

Iran flew through the Asian World Cup qualifiers! They easily won Group A with 16 points from eight games, including home and away wins against closest rivals South Korea! Nobody could stop them!

STAR MAN! Ashkan Dejagah

STRENGTH!

Iran have a great team spirit and their defence was absolutely unbreakable in qualifying!

WEAKNESS!

Reza Ghoochannejhad is a decent striker, but Iran will still struggle to score goals at this level!

STRONGEST STARTING XI!

Ahmadi — Sepahan

Heydari — Esteghlal
Hosseini — Persepolis
Montazeri — Umm-Salal
Beikzadeh — Esteghlal

Teymourian — Esteghlal
Nekounam — Al-Kuwait

Dejagah — Fulham
Jabbari — Al Ahli
Shojaei — Las Palmas

Ghoochannejhad — Charlton

SUPER SUBS: Davari, Lak, Mahini, Sadeghi, Hajsafi, Zare, Ebrahimi, Pooladi, Rezaei, Ansarifard, Azmoun, Hatami.

IRAN'S HEROES!

PENALTY KING
Javad Nekounam

SPEED MACHINE
Ashkan Dejagah

MUSCLEMAN
Pejman Montazeri

WONDERKID
Sardar Azmoun

MATCH VERDICT!

Iran could frustrate teams with their defensive tactics, but we don't think they've got the firepower to trouble Argentina, Nigeria or Bosnia & Herzegovina. A group stage exit looks likely!

NIGERIA

| COACH | STEPHEN KESHI | WORLD RANKING | 41ST | WORLD CUP ODDS | 300/1 | WORLD CUP BEST | LAST 16 1994 & 1998 |

QUALIFYING FORM!

The Super Eagles joined the African section of World Cup qualifying in round two and bossed Group F! That sent them through to the third round, where they beat Ethiopia 4-1 on aggregate to reach Brazil!

STAR MAN! Victor Moses

STRENGTH!

Nigeria's speedsters can rip teams apart! Victor Moses, Ahmed Musa and Nnamdi Oduamadi are rapid!

WEAKNESS!

Their front six are class, but The Super Eagles seriously lack big game experience in defence!

STRONGEST STARTING XI!

Enyeama — Lille

Ambrose — Celtic
Egwuekwe — Warri Wolves
Oboabona — Caykur Rizespor
Elderson — Monaco

Onazi — Lazio
Mikel — Chelsea

Musa — CSKA Moscow
Moses — Liverpool
Ideye — Dynamo Kiev

Emenike — Fenerbahce

SUPER SUBS: Ejide, Agbim, Kwambe, Omeruo, Okwuosa, Benjamin, Mba, Oduamadi, Igiebor, Uche, Ameobi, Obinna.

NIGERIA'S HEROES!

PENALTY KING
Victor Moses

SPEED MACHINE
Nnamdi Oduamadi

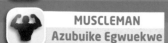
MUSCLEMAN
Azubuike Egwuekwe

WONDERKID
Ahmed Musa

MATCH VERDICT!

Nigeria are full of electric pace and raw power, but we don't think their defence will be able to handle strikers like Messi, Higuain, Aguero and Dzeko! They'll struggle to finish in the top two!

BIG '10

Test your knowledge on the class teams in Groups E and F by tackling these brainbusters!

1 How many goals did Lionel Messi score at the last World Cup in 2010?

2 Switzerland were the only team to beat which massive country at the 2010 World Cup?

3 Honduras play their first Group E game against which European country?

4 For which Group E country does Man. United winger Antonio Valencia play?

5 Bosnia & Herzegovina midfielder Miralem Pjanic plays for which Serie A club?

6 Name Liverpool's loan star who plays for Group F heroes Nigeria!

7 When did Argentina last win the World Cup – 1986, 1990 or 1994?

8 Which footy legend managed Argentina at the 2010 World Cup?

9 France powerhouse Paul Pogba played for which Premier League team between 2009 and 2012?

10 Which rock-solid Prem superstar is Bosnia & Herzegovina's goalkeeper?

FENAFUTH
Federación Nacional Autónoma de Fútbol de Honduras

ANSWERS ON PAGE 90

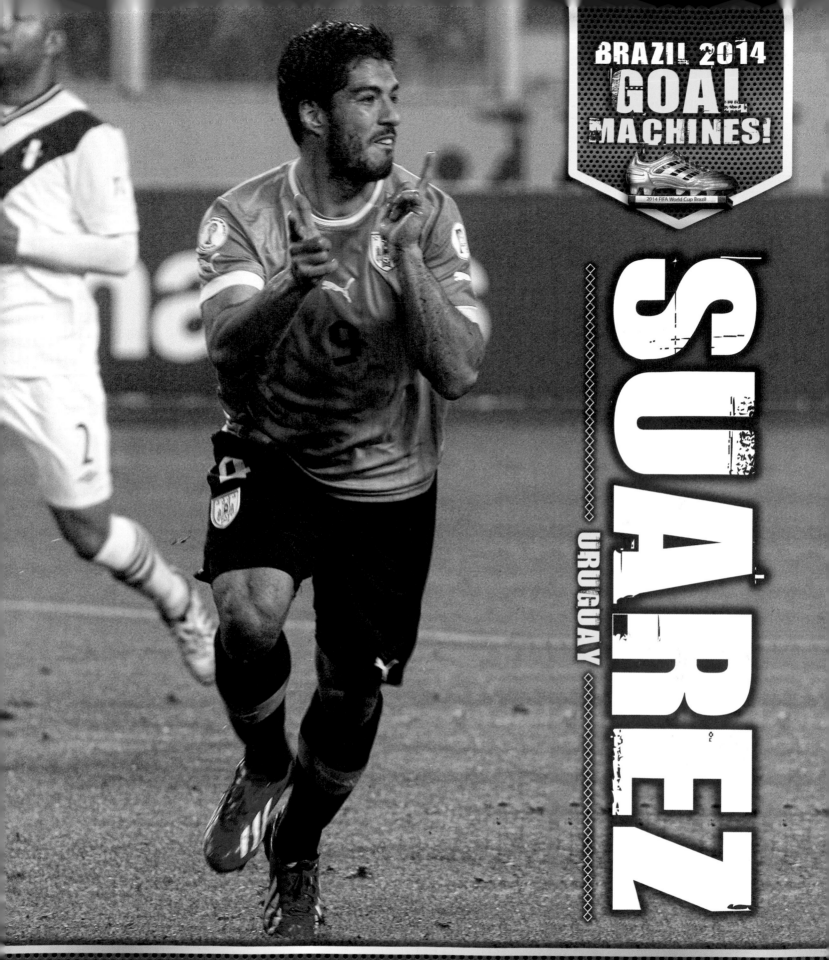

SUAREZ

URUGUAY

Luis finished as top scorer in South America's World Cup 2014 qualifying section with 11 goals – more than Messi, Falcao and Aguero!

Suarez took just 15 games to score 20 Prem goals in 2013-14 and reached the mark by January 1 – both are Premier League records!

He produced one of the best individual displays in qualifying after bagging four goals in Uruguay's 4-0 crushing of Chile in November 2011!

GERMANY

COACH JOACHIM LOW

CAPTAIN PHILIPP LAHM

MOST CAPS MIROSLAV KLOSE 130

QUALIFYING FORM!

Germany sailed through Group C in Europe's qualifying section! They won nine games out of ten, and only dropped points when they bizarrely drew 4-4 with Sweden after leading 4-0! Mesut Ozil netted eight goals in the group, Marco Reus bagged five, and Thomas Muller, Miroslav Klose, Andre Schurrle and Mario Gotze all scored four!

THE TACTICS!

Joachim Low uses a 4-2-3-1 system, with the full-backs bombing forward and Bastian Schweinsteiger holding in midfield. He sometimes plays Ozil, Reus or Gotze as a false No.9, but legendary hitman Klose should start the tournament up front!

Philipp Lahm

STRENGTH!

After years of gelling together and learning a new style of play, Germany look like they're finally hitting their peak as a team!

WEAKNESS!

They'll badly miss the tough tackling, drive and power of injured defensive midfielder Sami Khedira, while Klose might be too old to dominate the tournament's top centre-backs!

STAR MAN!

MESUT OZIL
ARSENAL

CAPS: 52 **GOALS:** 17

The Arsenal playmaker is the most expensive German player of all time, and the star that makes this team tick! Ozil has created the most chances in European club football over the last five seasons and can unlock any defence in a second with his supreme vision!

| MOST GOALS | MIROSLAV KLOSE 68 | WORLD RANKING | 2ND | WORLD CUP ODDS | 11/2 | WORLD CUP BEST | WINNERS 1954, 1974 & 1990 |

WATCH OUT FOR...

MARCO REUS
BORUSSIA DORTMUND

CAPS: 19 **GOALS:** 7

The Dortmund forward is nicknamed 'Rolls Reus' for his lightning pace and silky skills! His epic form helped Dortmund reach the Champions League final last year and the best is yet to come! He's pure class!

LAST FIVE RESULTS!

Sep. 10 2013	Faroe Islands	0-3	Germany
			Mertesacker 22, Ozil 74 (pen), Muller 84
Oct. 11 2013	Germany	3-0	Rep. Of Ireland
	Khedira 12, Schurrle 58, Ozil 90		
Oct. 15 2013	Sweden	3-5	Germany
	Hysen 6, 69, Kacaniklic 42		Ozil 45, Gotze 53, Schurrle 57, 66, 76
Nov. 15 2013	Italy	1-1	Germany
	Abate 28		Hummels 8
Nov. 19 2013	England	0-1	Germany
			Mertesacker 39

STRONGEST STARTING XI!

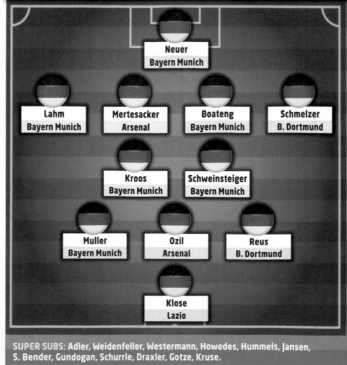

Neuer
Bayern Munich

Lahm
Bayern Munich

Mertesacker
Arsenal

Boateng
Bayern Munich

Schmelzer
B. Dortmund

Kroos
Bayern Munich

Schweinsteiger
Bayern Munich

Muller
Bayern Munich

Ozil
Arsenal

Reus
B. Dortmund

Klose
Lazio

SUPER SUBS: Adler, Weidenfeller, Westermann, Howedes, Hummels, Jansen, S. Bender, Gundogan, Schurrle, Draxler, Gotze, Kruse.

GERMANY'S HEROES!

PENALTY KING
Mesut Ozil

SPEED MACHINE
Marco Reus

MUSCLEMAN
Mats Hummels

WONDERKID
Julian Draxler

MATCH VERDICT!

Germany have reached the semi-finals at every major tournament since 2006, but this could be the year they go one step further! We think they'll reach the final, but will end up second best!

PORTUGAL

COACH	PAULO BENTO	WORLD RANKING	5TH	WORLD CUP ODDS	28/1	WORLD CUP BEST	THIRD PLACE 1966

QUALIFYING FORM!

Portugal had a shaky journey to Brazil. They finished second behind Russia in Europe's Group F, and drew Sweden in the play-offs. Cristiano Ronaldo bagged the only goal in the first leg, before sealing a 4-2 aggregate win with a slick hat-trick in the second leg!

Joao Moutinho

STAR MAN!

CRISTIANO RONALDO
REAL MADRID

CAPS: 109 **GOALS:** 47

Not many experts think Portugal have a chance of lifting the famous trophy this summer, but we reckon they can beat any opponent when C-Ron's on form! He scored 69 goals in 59 games in 2013, and has the skills to win matches all by himself!

STRENGTH!

Any team with the FIFA Ballon d'Or winner in their XI must be feared. Ronaldo can destroy any defence!

WEAKNESS!

If Ron has an off day or teams man-mark him out of the game, Portugal sometimes struggle to hit the net!

LAST FIVE RESULTS!

Date	Home	Score	Away
Sep. 11 2013	Brazil — Silva 24, Neymar 34, Jo 49	3-1	Portugal — Meireles 18
Oct. 11 2013	Portugal — Costa 27	1-1	Israel — Ben Basat 85
Oct. 15 2013	Portugal — Varela 30, Nani 36, Postiga 79	3-0	Luxembourg
Nov. 15 2013	Portugal — Ronaldo 82	1-0	Sweden
Nov. 19 2013	Sweden — Ibrahimovic 68, 72	2-3	Portugal — Ronaldo 50, 77, 79

STRONGEST STARTING XI!

Patricio — Sporting Lisbon

Pereira — Valencia
Pepe — Real Madrid
Bruno Alves — Fenerbahce
Coentrao — Real Madrid

Meireles — Fenerbahce
Veloso — Dynamo Kiev

Nani — Man. United
Moutinho — Monaco
Ronaldo — Real Madrid

Postiga — Lazio

SUPER SUBS: Eduardo, Beto, A. Almeida, Costa, Neto, Antunes, Micael, Josue, W. Carvalho, Varela, H. Almeida, Eder.

PORTUGAL'S HEROES!

PENALTY KING — Cristiano Ronaldo

SPEED MACHINE — Cristiano Ronaldo

MUSCLEMAN — Bruno Alves

WONDERKID — William Carvalho

VERDICT!

Portugal might have the most in-form star on the planet, but they don't have many extra options in attack! They could go far if Ronaldo brings his A-game, but we think they'll get knocked out in the last 16!

 germany
 portugal
 ghana
 usa

GHANA

| COACH | AKWASI APPIAH | WORLD RANKING | 24TH | WORLD CUP ODDS | 150/1 | WORLD CUP BEST | QUARTER FINALS 2010 |

QUALIFYING FORM!

Ghana started their campaign in round two of the African qualifying section and won Group D with 15 points! They were drawn against Egypt in round three, and reached Brazil with a big 7-3 aggregate win!

STAR MAN! Andre Ayew

STRENGTH!

Ghana rock in midfield! Teams won't like facing Kwadwo Asamoah, Andre Ayew and Kevin-Prince Boateng!

WEAKNESS!

None of their defenders play in the top five European leagues! Can they stop players like Ronaldo and Reus?

STRONGEST STARTING XI!

Dauda — Orlando Pirates
Opare — Standard Liege
Sumaila — M. Sundowns
Akaminko — Eskisehirspor
Inkoom — Platanias
Essien — AC Milan
A. Ayew — Marseille
Muntari — AC Milan
Boateng — Schalke
Asamoah — Juventus
Gyan — Al-Ain

SUPER SUBS: Kwarasey, Kingson, Awal, Afful, Addy, Gyimah, Agyemang-Badu, Mubarak, Adomah, Atsu, J. Ayew, Waris.

GHANA'S HEROES!

 PENALTY KING Asamoah Gyan

 SPEED MACHINE Christian Atsu

 MUSCLEMAN Michael Essien

 WONDERKID Majeed Waris

MATCH VERDICT!

Ghana's attacking midfielders should help them score goals past their Group G rivals and striker Asamoah Gyan loves the World Cup, but we don't think they can stop Germany and Portugal from qualifying!

USA

| COACH | JURGEN KLINSMANN | WORLD RANKING | 14TH | WORLD CUP ODDS | 200/1 | WORLD CUP BEST | THIRD PLACE 1930 |

QUALIFYING FORM!

USA qualified from the six-team, round four CONCACAF group in first place with 22 points! They finished four points ahead of rivals Costa Rica, and Jozy Altidore was their top scorer with four goals!

STAR MAN! Clint Dempsey

STRENGTH!

Jermaine Jones and Michael Bradley protect the defence, while Tim Howard is a top shot-stopper!

WEAKNESS!

They struggled to score against average teams in qualifying, so they'll find it even tougher in Brazil!

STRONGEST STARTING XI!

Howard — Everton
Cameron — Stoke
Gonzalez — LA Galaxy
Besler — Kansas City
Beasley — Puebla
Jones — Besiktas
Bradley — Toronto
Bedoya — Nantes
Dempsey — Seattle Sounders
Donovan — LA Galaxy
Altidore — Sunderland

SUPER SUBS: Guzan, Rimando, Evans, Orozco, Goodson, Castillo, Diskerud, Kljestan, Zusi, E. Johnson, Johannsson, Boyd.

USA'S HEROES!

 PENALTY KING Clint Dempsey

 SPEED MACHINE DaMarcus Beasley

 MUSCLEMAN Jermaine Jones

 WONDERKID Terrence Boyd

MATCH VERDICT!

USA qualified easily and gaffer Jurgen Klinsmann has created an awesome team spirit. But they've been handed a rock-hard draw, so we'd be shocked if they reached the last 16!

BELGIUM

| COACH | MARC WILMOTS | CAPTAIN | VINCENT KOMPANY | MOST CAPS | DANIEL VAN BUYTEN 76 |

QUALIFYING FORM!

Belgium totally rocked in European qualification, winning a national record seven games on the trot to top Group A! They finished the campaign undefeated, hit 18 goals, conceded just four and outclassed the likes of Croatia and Serbia!

THE TACTICS!

Belgium play a 4-2-3-1 formation with the two holding midfielders, allowing Eden Hazard, Kevin de Bruyne and Kevin Mirallas to supply chances for Christian Benteke or Romelu Lukaku. But even though they've got skill to burn, they're a strong team who have built their success on a watertight defence!

Vincent Kompany

STRENGTH!

The Red Devils' attackers love ripping teams to shreds with their pace and tricks, with the wide men supplying the strikers or cutting in themselves for shots at goal!

WEAKNESS!

Belgium's wingers are great going forward, but they sometimes leave full-backs Toby Alderweireld and Jan Vertonghen, who are more-suited at centre-back, exposed!

STAR MAN!

EDEN HAZARD
CHELSEA

Caps: 42 **Goals:** 5

Hazard is a defender's nightmare – he loves dribbling at rapid pace, can change direction quickly and is hard to knock off the ball! He's been criticised for not scoring enough or tracking back, but he's improved both this season with Chelsea and will be totally unstoppable in Brazil!

WATCH OUT FOR...

THIBAUT COURTOIS
ATLETICO MADRID

CAPS: 14 **GOALS:** 0

Chelsea's reserve keeper is on loan at Atletico Madrid this season and is quickly earning a reputation as a world-class player! His reflexes are razor-sharp and he's a quality shot-stopper!

LAST FIVE RESULTS!

Sep. 6 2013	Scotland	0-2	Belgium
Oct. 11 2013	Croatia	1-2	Belgium
Oct. 15 2013	Belgium	1-1	Wales
Nov. 14 2013	Belgium	0-2	Colombia
Nov. 19 2013	Belgium	2-3	Japan

Scotland 0-2 Belgium — Defour 38, Mirallas 88
Croatia 1-2 Belgium — Kranjcar 83; Lukaku 15, 38
Belgium 1-1 Wales — De Bruyne 64; Ramsey 88
Belgium 0-2 Colombia — Falcao 51, Ibarbo 66
Belgium 2-3 Japan — Mirallas 15, Alderweireld 79; Kakitani 37, Honda 53, Okazaki 63

STRONGEST STARTING XI!

Courtois — Atletico Madrid

Alderweireld — Atletico Madrid
Van Buyten — Bayern Munich
Kompany — Man. City
Vertonghen — Tottenham

Witsel — Zenit
Dembele — Tottenham

Mirallas — Everton
De Bruyne — Wolfsburg
Hazard — Chelsea

Benteke — Aston Villa

SUPER SUBS: Mignolet, Casteels, Meunier, Lombaerts, Vermaelen, Fellaini, Defour, Chadli, Mertens, Bakkali, Lukaku, Vossen.

BELGIUM'S HEROES!

 PENALTY KING Eden Hazard

 SPEED MACHINE Kevin Mirallas

 MUSCLEMAN Christian Benteke

 WONDERKID Zakaria Bakkali

MATCH VERDICT!

MATCH reckons Belgium could rock the World Cup! They've got loads of young attacking stars and a tough defence! We're tipping them to top Group H and at least reach the quarter-finals!

RUSSIA

COACH	FABIO CAPELLO	WORLD RANKING	22ND	WORLD CUP ODDS	66/1	WORLD CUP BEST	FOURTH PLACE 1966

STAR MAN!

IGOR AKINFEEV
CSKA MOSCOW

Caps: 65 **Goals:** 0

Akinfeev made his debut for Russia as an 18-year-old and people raved about his potential! Injuries held him back in the past, but he played every minute of the qualifiers and made tons of top saves! If he has a big tournament, Russia could go far!

QUALIFYING FORM!

Despite back-to-back defeats to Portugal and Northern Ireland, Russia still managed to top Europe's Group F by a point. Their home form was mind-blowing – they hit 11 goals, conceded just two and won all five qualifiers on their own turf!

Roman Shirokov

STRENGTH!

Fabio Capello has made Russia hard to score against. They conceded just five goals in ten qualifiers!

WEAKNESS!

They lack a truly world-class striker. Zenit hitman Aleksandr Kerzhakov is their main man in attack, but he's yet to do it on the big stage!

LAST FIVE RESULTS!

Sep. 10 2013	**Russia** V. Berezutski 49, Kokorin 52, Glushakov 74	**3-1**	Israel Zahavi 90
Oct. 11 2013	Luxembourg	**0-4**	**Russia** Samedov 9, Fayzulin 39, Glushakov 45, Kerzhakov 73
Oct. 15 2013	Azerbaijan Javadov 90	**1-1**	**Russia** Shirokov 16
Nov. 15 2013	**Russia** Samedov 30	**1-1**	Serbia F. Djordjevic 31
Nov. 19 2013	**Russia** Smolov 12, Tarasov 59	**2-1**	South Korea Shin-Wook Kim 6

STRONGEST STARTING XI!

Akinfeev CSKA Moscow

Kozlov Kuban Krasnodar
V. Berezutski CSKA Moscow
Ignashevich CSKA Moscow
Kombarov Spartak Moscow

Shirokov Zenit
Denisov Dynamo Moscow
Fayzulin Zenit

Bystrov Anzhi
Kerzhakov Zenit
Kokorin Dynamo Moscow

SUPER SUBS: Gabulov, Lodygin, Anyukov, Granat, Yeshchenko, Zhirkov, Glushakov, Tarasov, Samedov, Dzagoev, Smolov, Cheryshev.

RUSSIA'S HEROES!

PENALTY KING Roman Shirokov

SPEED MACHINE Vladimir Bystrov

MUSCLEMAN Sergei Ignashevich

WONDERKID Aleksandr Kokorin

MATCH VERDICT!

Russia should have way too much quality for South Korea and Algeria and finish second in Group H. But the lack of a top-class goalscorer will be costly, and we reckon they'll bomb out in the last 16!

belgium   algeria   russia   korea republic

SOUTH KOREA

| COACH | MYUNG-BO HONG | WORLD RANKING | 53RD | WORLD CUP ODDS | 250/1 | WORLD CUP BEST | FOURTH PLACE 2002 |

QUALIFYING FORM!

South Korea grabbed second spot ahead of Uzbekistan on goal difference in Asian Group A. But rubbish performances at home to Iran and away in Lebanon saw their coach Kang-Hee Choi resign!

STAR MAN! Heung-Min Son

STRENGTH!

The South Koreans know what it's like to play at the World Cup finals – this is their eighth in a row!

WEAKNESS!

New manager Myung-Bo Hong has been experimenting with his side, so they don't have a settled XI!

STRONGEST STARTING XI!

Sung-Ryong Jung
Suwon Bluewings

Chang-Soo Kim
Kashiwa Reysol

Tae-Hwi Kwak
Al-Hilal

Jeong-Ho Hong
Augsburg

Chi-Woo Kim
FC Seoul

Keun-Ho Lee
Sangju Sangmu

Sung-Yueng Ki
Sunderland

Bo-Kyung Kim
Cardiff

Heung-Min Son
B. Leverkusen

Dong-Gook Lee
Jeonbuk Hyundai

Dong-Won Ji
Augsburg

SUPER SUBS: Seung-Gyu Kim, Bum-Young Lee, Hyo-Jin Choi, Young-Gwon Kim, Kee-Hee Kim, Joo-Ho Park, Myung-Joo Lee, Jong-Woo Park, Chung-Yong Lee, Ja-Cheol Koo, Shin-Wook Kim, Ju-Young Park.

SOUTH KOREA'S HEROES!

PENALTY KING
Sung-Yueng Ki

SPEED MACHINE
Heung-Min Son

MUSCLEMAN
Tae-Hwi Kwak

WONDERKID
Heung-Min Son

MATCH VERDICT!

South Korea reached the semis when they hosted the World Cup with Japan back in 2002. But they're not as good as they used to be, so we're predicting an early exit for Myung-Bo Hong's side!

ALGERIA

| COACH | VAHID HALILHODZIC | WORLD RANKING | 27TH | WORLD CUP ODDS | 1,000/1 | WORLD CUP BEST | GROUP STAGE 1982, 1986 & 2010 |

QUALIFYING FORM!

Algeria bossed Africa's Group H – they won five of their six games and Islam Slimani hit five goals! That sealed a play-off with Burkina Faso, where a 1-0 win in the second leg put them through on away goals!

STAR MAN! Sofiane Feghouli

STRENGTH!

Silky attackers Saphir Taider, El Arbi Hillel Soudani and Sofiane Feghouli can carve defences wide open!

WEAKNESS!

The majority of their squad lacks big-game experience, and that could cost them on the big stage!

STRONGEST STARTING XI!

Zemmamouche
USM Alger

Mostefa
Ajaccio

Bougherra
Lekhwiya

Belkalem
Watford

Mesbah
Livorno

Guedioura
Crystal Palace

Medjani
Valenciennes

Feghouli
Valencia

Taider
Inter Milan

Soudani
Dinamo Zagreb

Slimani
Sporting Lisbon

SUPER SUBS: M'Bolhi, Si Mohamed, Cadamuro-Bentaiba, Rial, Ghoulam, Khoualed, Lacen, Yebda, Kadir, Brahimi, Djebbour, Belfodil.

ALGERIA'S HEROES!

PENALTY KING
Saphir Taider

SPEED MACHINE
Sofiane Feghouli

MUSCLEMAN
Madjid Bougherra

WONDERKID
Saphir Taider

MATCH VERDICT!

Algeria are ranked well above South Korea, but it's a battle between those two to avoid bottom spot! They've got some decent players, but we can't see the African side troubling Belgium or Russia!

BIG MATCH! QUIZ

WORLD CUP SPECIAL!

MATCH! WINNER!

Who scored the only goal of the game in England's 1-0 win over Slovenia at World Cup 2010?

5 QUESTIONS ON...

SERGIO AGUERO

1 The lethal goal machine started his career at which Argentinian club – River Plate or Independiente?

2 True or False? Aguero used to play alongside Chelsea striker Fernando Torres at Atletico Madrid!

3 How much did Man. City pay to sign Kun from Atletico Madrid in 2011 – £28 million or £38 million?

4 Which Argentina legend is Aguero's son's godfather – Diego Maradona, Ossie Ardiles, Gonzalo Higuain or Lionel Messi?

5 How old will the legendary striker be when the World Cup kicks off on June 12 – 26, 27 or 28?

FIFA 14 CHALLENGE!

Name the Chelsea FUT superstars who could be busting out their skills in Brazil this summer!

85	LM
87 PAC	88 DRI
79 SHO	48 DEF
83 PAS	62 HEA

77	RB
78 PAC	72 DRI
57 SHO	77 DEF
76 PAS	68 HEA

1.

2.

SOCCER SCRABBLE

Rearrange these letters to find a red-hot World Cup 2014 goal machine!

N P N E R I I
O A
I V B E R

SPOT THE BALL!

Mark where you think the ball should be in this action pic!

Rows: A B C D E F G H I J K

Columns: 1 2 3 4 5 6 7 8 9 10 11 12 13 14 15 16 17 18 19

These teams play their first World Cup game in which stadium?

1 Manaus	2 Maracana	3 Salvador	4 Porto Alegre

A England	B France	C Spain	D Argentina

TRUE or FALSE?

Read these statements and work out if they're true or false!

1. Football legends Brazil have won the World Cup a record six times!

2. The 2002 World Cup was hosted by France with the final being held in Paris!

3. No European country has ever won the World Cup outside of Europe!

4. England star Wayne Rooney was sent off against Portugal at World Cup 2006!

5. RVP scored the winner as Holland beat Spain 1-0 in the 2010 World Cup Final!

ANSWERS ON PAGE 90

MUSCLE MAN!

PERFORMED BY: Cristiano Ronaldo
The Ballon d'Or winner knows how good he is – he points to himself after every goal!

I'M THE BEST!

GOAL

PARTY TIME!

PERFORMED BY: Asamoah Gyan
Nobody loves a goal celebration more than Ghana hero Asamoah Gyan. He dances like a funky robot!

PERFORMED BY: Mario Balotelli
The Italy superstar reckons he's The Incredible Hulk when he rips his shirt off!

THE SOMERSAULT!

PERFORMED BY: Nani
The Portugal winger's going to hurt himself doing this one day! He flips around like an Olympic gymnast!

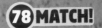

CORNER FLAG CRUSHER!

PERFORMED BY:
Tim Cahill

Australia might not score this summer, but Cahill will be punching the nearest corner flag if they do!

CRAZY!

Get ready to see some awesome goal celebrations in Brazil!

RIDE THE WAVE!

PERFORMED BY:
Daniel Sturridge

England fans would love to see Sturridge show off his famous dance in Brazil! His arms are all over the place!

THE SKY POINTER!

PERFORMED BY:
Christian Benteke

The Belgium bulldozer celebrates every goal by pointing both fingers towards the sky!

CLASSIC MOVES!

Check out these iconic celebrations from the World Cup archive!

TARDELLI!

Italy legend Marco Tardelli scored in the 1982 World Cup Final and sprinted away in tears!

SOUTH AFRICA!

The 2010 hosts busted out this dance after scoring the opening goal at the last World Cup!

SCOTTI!

Andres Scotti celebrated Uruguay's 2010 quarter-final win by putting on a duck costume!

MILLA!

Cameroon legend Roger Milla couldn't stop dancing in front of corner flags at Italia '90!

```
K Q S V C M H Y                                                    L Z O K E Z D T
O Z M Z H Z W S                                                    R O I A K X I L
P R Z R O C Z C                                                    P N V Y P H L X
U T X O N A X W                                                    V M V U M B L B
A M I O W G C X                                                    A Y N X K Z I A
I A O D E R G E N S G S D B M Z P C D D F C C J B L P D Y D X V E I Q
K E C Q T W F X Q Z X Y P N P T O F T P L M F V C B I Q Q W N A O Q
I H K S J I D U Q J R Y P Z E W Q H A P T X X U N E R G S J C E C X M
I H V F Q R D H J N G F X T Y G I R V P W G P N K W W B R Q A E Y X R
W I Y C A T E M I J F H I S E N S W M K G F B J Q A H N I A U G I H B
D R B Z Z F R U N Y S L N E H T D H P G S K R D I W K U V U D H M C A B
V L A I G V F F J G S U O B B F R N C H G J K U P S T U R R I D G E A M
G H O I J R K G W R S D E L L N S D L A Z C A V A N I T L J H L Y I T K
A I E B N F A L C A O V M S L T C Y F Q T O M Y Z H N W V Z O G L M M J
D R R Z D K X Y T V                                                Y D A D P K D M Z M
P F O P A R Y F S L                                                A R N I Y C F Y E I
I V H L I T W B Q X                                                U S P A H P P P T G
I P L W E Z I S M S                                                H I E G A W F D M L
F Z F D G Y P N Z M                                                C M R C B D R G E L
M V K W Z X W Z W H                                                M O S U G U O M I Z
Z Z Z V V O T X C P                                                T D I A D Q W Z E Y
U A L F L C U N I P                                                V G E L L M S I S O
I X O F W D V X F T                                                Y E N O O R X D K K
S K U H Z I Y P O R                                                F P H D D W P G E E
G U F O H J Y K U D                                                X T J C O C V G A P
T F I K N Y L Y J N                                                H L P K U H M H J O
C X L R F P C D F Z                                                I C F G R L K M G R
M Z E D N A N R E H                                                W Z Q Q F G I M X A
I A V L A D Z W Z Y                                                D M A R T I N E Z V
W F H G Z D A Z Q D                                                S P J R G S A E N P
I D J N U I F V F U M Z H K L T J C X Q T O R R E S U D S Q W V O I X K
R G F Q S Q Z X K O Q C T M U L L E R R Q F Z G J Z A X H Z S E Q D H A
P E G S Z Y K E A R G D D E B L U N N O D C L E C M R Z I B J Y U Q H S
W C E P J O R Q W I U W W E S B K E N N C O B I M Y E Q R V B A E J D
H M G B Y Z F U Y G U F U X D Q R E O A G R O D P H Z X L G E G D R G R
E S B N H U V D D O Y U S O O M Y T I L Z Z B C O Y E F I B I U Y R R K
G W F A L C S E W N L L P A M M L X Z D P E W A Z E H I V M Y E R Q V G
G W K H R B Q L D E T X L E A K N N B O Z U M P K Q C E J U P R O Y X G
V O H I Q V M S K E I M R Y T D A T S O C Y U G E N L Y Z M O B C W I
V S V H F T W X Q D R X I U Z X F C B E N Z E M A B A H H R H M B D Y V
Z U M X F P F O T V D B E N T E K E T L I A Z N A F S V S U L E O A A
H W F J R B L H I J D T C Y H O J T T E X A Z V X V A L F U L V N V S J
R K A W T N N Y O R V U X O T Z E L K D D T W A V D Z D N K J B E K E
```

Aguero
Balotelli
Benteke
Benzema
Cavani

Costa
Dzeko
Falcao
Fred
Giroud

Hazard
Hernandez
Higuain
Hulk
Kerzhakov

Lukaku
Martinez
Messi
Muller
Negredo

Neymar
Reus
Robben
Ronaldo
Rooney

Sanchez
Sturridge
Suarez
Torres
Van Persie

ANSWERS ON PAGE 90

BENZEMA

FRANCE

Benzema scored the fastest ever El Clasico goal when he netted after ten seconds against Barça on December 10, 2011! Wow!

The wicked striker was named French Player Of The Year two years in a row in 2011 and 2012! He won the Ligue 1 Player Of The Year award in 2008, too!

The awesome France superstar bagged his 100th goal for Real Madrid in a 5-0 win away to Real Betis earlier this year! He loves ripping net!

WORLD CUP

LEGENDS

MATCH picks the best XI players from World Cup finals history!

DIEGO MARADONA

ST

WORLD CUPS

1982, 1986, 1990 & 1994

No footy star has ever dominated a single tournament more than Maradona did in 1986! He bagged five goals and five assists to help Argentina win the World Cup, including a famous double against England in the quarter-finals!

ZINEDINE ZIDANE

CM

WORLD CUPS

1998, 2002 & 2006

Zizou became the most famous footy star on the planet after scoring twice in the 1998 World Cup Final! His double helped France win the tournament, and he nearly inspired a second win in 2006 with a series of stunning performances!

MANAGER SIR ALF RAMSEY

WORLD CUPS

1966 & 1970

Ramsey is a legend for helping England win the World Cup in 1966! One of his greatest moments was sticking with striker Geoff Hurst for the final against West Germany - he ended up hitting a match-winning hat-trick! Ramsey was a genius!

ANDREAS BREHME

LB

WORLD CUPS

1986, 1990 & 1994

Brehme was two-footed, competitive, tough-tackling, powerful, passionate, intelligent and a dead-ball demon! The rampaging left-back became a German legend in 1990, as his late penalty helped his country beat Argentina 1-0 in the final!

FRANZ BECKENBAUER

CB

WORLD CUPS

1966, 1970 & 1974

The Kaiser's the most famous defender in footy history! He invented the role of the sweeper and was one of the first defenders to have the technical skills of a midfielder! His display in the 1974 World Cup Final for West Germany is legendary!

PELE

WORLD CUPS

1958, 1962, 1966 & 1970

ST

No World Cup Legends XI is complete without Pele! The Brazil hero is the most famous footy star of all time and a true legend of the game! He made history by winning the trophy as a 17-year-old in 1958, then owned another World Cup in 1970!

RONALDO

WORLD CUPS

1994, 1998, 2002 & 2006

ST

When you hear the name Ronaldo, you probably think of a Portugal star, but the original version was just as good! The rapid striker's 15 goals in the three tournaments he played at make him the top scorer in World Cup history!

SUBSTITUTES

OLIVER KAHN GK	
CARLOS ALBERTO RB	
FABIO CANNAVARO CB	
SIR BOBBY CHARLTON CM	
GARRINCHA RW	
GERD MULLER ST	
EUSEBIO ST	

LOTHAR MATTHAUS

WORLD CUPS

1982, 1986, 1990, 1994 & 1998

CM

Matthaus has played 25 games at the World Cup, which is an all-time record! He's also one of only two stars to play at FIVE different tournaments! More importantly, his legendary displays helped West Germany go all the way in 1990!

JOHAN CRUYFF

WORLD CUPS

1974

CM

Holland weren't famous before the 1974 tournament, but Cruyff made them the coolest team on the planet! One of the most naturally-gifted players ever, he was at the heart of their 'Total Football' style which saw them go all the way to the final!

DINO ZOFF

WORLD CUPS

1970, 1974, 1978 & 1982

GK

The Italy legend is one of the greatest goalkeepers ever! His finest moment arrived at the 1982 tournament in Spain. Aged 40, he became the oldest ever player to win the World Cup and the first goalkeeper to captain the winners!

BOBBY MOORE

WORLD CUPS

1962, 1966 & 1970

CB

Moore is an icon of English football and the captain for The Three Lions' only World Cup triumph in 1966! He wasn't lightning quick, but made up for it with incredible timing and positioning! Pele says he's the greatest defender he ever faced!

CAFU

WORLD CUPS

1994, 1998, 2002 & 2006

RB

Cafu is the most-capped Brazilian of all time and the only player to play in three World Cup finals! If you think Dani Alves is good, you should've seen Cafu at his peak! He bombed up and down the wing all day long, and was unstoppable at World Cup 2002!

ROAD TO THE

Can you go all the way from the World Cup group stages to the final before your

9

10
Maradona played for which country?
Right – Move forward one space!
Wrong – Move back two spaces!

21

22

8

11

20

23
Gary Medel plays for which country?
Right – Move forward two spaces!
Wrong – Move back three spaces!

7
You've won your opening game 2-1 in Belo Horizonte! Move forward four spaces!

12
You've cruised to another victory in the group stages! Move forward one space!

19
What is this year's World Cup ball called?
Right – Move forward three spaces!
Wrong – Move back five spaces!

24

START!
You've qualified for the World Cup! The highest roll goes first!
↓ ↓ ↓ ↓

6

13

18
You've smashed home a stunning hat-trick in a group game! Move forward three spaces!

25

2

5
You've lost your opening group game 3-0 in Sao Paulo! Move back three spaces!

14

17

26
You've finished top of your group and are heading for the last 16! Move forward four spaces!

3

4
Who's older – David Luiz or Thiago Silva?
Right – Move forward two spaces!
Wrong – Move back two spaces!

15
You've missed an absolute sitter in a group game! Move back four spaces!

16

27
What country hosted World Cup 2010?
Right – Move forward one space!
Wrong – Move back two spaces!

MATCH!
THE BEST FOOTBALL MAGAZINE!

MARACANA!

rivals? Use coins as counters, grab a dice and battle your mates in this epic game!

30	**31** You've scored the winning goal in a last 16 clash! Move forward three spaces!	**42**	**43**	**WINNER!** Congratulations! You've reached the World Cup Final at The Maracana!
29 Noooooo! You've been knocked out of the group stages! Move back nine spaces!	**32**	**41**	**44** Which country won World Cup 2010? Right – Move forward two spaces! Wrong – Move back three spaces!	**49** Name the last World Cup winning hosts! Right – Move forward one space! Wrong – Move back 11 spaces!
28	**33**	**40**	**45** You're sent off in the fifth minute of the World Cup semi-finals! Move back four spaces!	**48**
34	**39** You've set up the winning goal in the quarter-finals! Move forward three spaces!	**46**	**47** You've scored a 30-yard screamer in the World Cup semi-finals! Move forward one space!
35 Kevin Strootman plays for which club? Right – Move forward three spaces! Wrong – Move back five spaces!	**38**		
36	**37** Your country are 1-0 down in the quarter-finals and you hit the post! Move back seven spaces!		

MATCH! THE BEST FOOTBALL MAGAZINE!

ANSWERS!

4, Thiago Silva;
10, Argentina;
19, Adidas Brazuca;
23, Chile;
27, South Africa;
35, Roma;
44, Spain;
49, France.

WORLD CUP 2014

Fill in the results for every game at Brazil 2014 this summer with

GROUP A — Brazil » Mexico » Cameroon » Croatia

Brazil	Croatia	Mexico	Cameroon
MATCH 1 June 12 ★ 9pm ITV ★ Sao Paulo Arena		**MATCH 2** June 13 ★ 5pm ITV ★ Das Dunas Arena	

Brazil	Mexico	Cameroon	Croatia
MATCH 17 June 17 ★ 8pm BBC ★ Castelao Stadium		**MATCH 18** June 18 ★ 11pm ITV ★ Amazonia Arena	

Cameroon	Brazil	Croatia	Mexico
MATCH 33 June 23 ★ 9pm ITV ★ Mane Garrincha		**MATCH 34** June 23 ★ 9pm ITV ★ Pernambuco Arena	

GROUP D — Uruguay » Costa Rica » England » Italy

Uruguay	Costa Rica	England	Italy
MATCH 7 June 14 ★ 8pm ITV ★ Castelao Stadium		**MATCH 8** June 14 ★ 11pm BBC ★ Amazonia Arena	

Uruguay	England	Italy	Costa Rica
MATCH 23 June 19 ★ 8pm ITV ★ Sao Paulo Arena		**MATCH 24** June 20 ★ 5pm BBC ★ Pernambuco Arena	

Italy	Uruguay	Costa Rica	England
MATCH 39 June 24 ★ 5pm ITV ★ Das Dunas Arena		**MATCH 40** June 24 ★ 5pm ITV ★ Mineirao Stadium	

GROUP B — Spain » Holland » Chile » Australia

Spain	Holland	Chile	Australia
MATCH 3 June 13 ★ 8pm BBC ★ Fonte Nova Arena		**MATCH 4** June 13 ★ 11pm ITV ★ Pantanal Arena	

Australia	Holland	Spain	Chile
MATCH 20 June 18 ★ 5pm ITV ★ Beira-Rio Stadium		**MATCH 19** June 18 ★ 8pm BBC ★ Maracana Stadium	

Australia	Spain	Holland	Chile
MATCH 35 June 23 ★ 5pm ITV ★ Da Baixada Arena		**MATCH 36** June 23 ★ 5pm ITV ★ Sao Paulo Arena	

Fred, Brazil

GROUP C — Colombia » Greece » Ivory Coast » Japan

Colombia	Greece	Ivory Coast	Japan
MATCH 5 June 14 ★ 5pm BBC ★ Mineirao Stadium		**MATCH 6** June 15 ★ 2am ITV ★ Pernambuco Arena	

Colombia	Ivory Coast	Japan	Greece
MATCH 21 June 19 ★ 5pm BBC ★ Mane Garrincha		**MATCH 22** June 19 ★ 11pm BBC ★ Das Dunas Arena	

Japan	Colombia	Greece	Ivory Coast
MATCH 37 June 24 ★ 9pm BBC ★ Pantanal Arena		**MATCH 38** June 24 ★ 9pm BBC ★ Castelao Stadium	

GROUP E — Switzerland » Ecuador » France » Honduras

Switzerland	Ecuador	France	Honduras
MATCH 9 June 15 ★ 5pm ITV ★ Mane Garrincha		**MATCH 10** June 15 ★ 8pm BBC ★ Beira-Rio Stadium	

Switzerland	France	Honduras	Ecuador
MATCH 25 June 20 ★ 8pm ITV ★ Fonte Nova Arena		**MATCH 26** June 20 ★ 11pm ITV ★ Da Baixada Arena	

Honduras	Switzerland	Ecuador	France
MATCH 41 June 25 ★ 9pm BBC ★ Amazonia Arena		**MATCH 42** June 25 ★ 9pm BBC ★ Maracana Stadium	

FIXTURES!

MATCH's epic World Cup fixtures guide!

FIFA WORLD CUP Brasil 2014

GROUP F — Argentina » Bosnia-Herz. » Iran » Nigeria

Argentina	Bosnia-H.		Iran	Nigeria
MATCH 11	June 15 ★ 11pm — BBC ★ Maracana Stadium		MATCH 12	June 16 ★ 8pm — BBC ★ Da Baixada Arena

Argentina	Iran		Nigeria	Bosnia-H.
MATCH 27	June 21 ★ 5pm — ITV ★ Mineirao Stadium		MATCH 28	June 21 ★ 11pm — BBC ★ Pantanal Arena

Nigeria	Argentina		Bosnia-H.	Iran
MATCH 43	June 25 ★ 5pm — ITV ★ Beira-Rio Stadium		MATCH 44	June 25 ★ 5pm — ITV ★ Fonte Nova Arena

GROUP G — Germany » Portugal » Ghana » USA

Germany	Portugal		Ghana	USA
MATCH 13	June 16 ★ 5pm — ITV ★ Fonte Nova Arena		MATCH 14	June 16 ★ 11pm — BBC ★ Das Dunas Arena

Germany	Ghana		USA	Portugal
MATCH 29	June 21 ★ 8pm — BBC ★ Castelao Stadium		MATCH 30	June 22 ★ 11pm — BBC ★ Amazonia Arena

USA	Germany		Portugal	Ghana
MATCH 45	June 26 ★ 5pm — BBC ★ Pernambuco Arena		MATCH 46	June 26 ★ 5pm — BBC ★ Mane Garrincha

GROUP H — Belgium » Algeria » Russia » South Korea

Belgium	Algeria		Russia	South Korea
MATCH 15	June 17 ★ 5pm — ITV ★ Mineirao Stadium		MATCH 16	June 17 ★ 11pm — BBC ★ Pantanal Arena

Belgium	Russia		South Korea	Algeria
MATCH 31	June 22 ★ 5pm — BBC ★ Maracana Stadium		MATCH 32	June 22 ★ 8pm — ITV ★ Beira-Rio Stadium

South Korea	Belgium		Algeria	Russia
MATCH 47	June 26 ★ 9pm — ITV ★ Sao Paulo Arena		MATCH 48	June 26 ★ 9pm — ITV ★ Da Baixada Arena

Nasri, France

Robben, Holland

Xavi, Spain

DAY-BY-DAY GUIDE!

June's gonna be packed with footy!

GROUP STAGE!

JUNE 12
Brazil v Croatia, Group A — ITV, 9pm

JUNE 13
Mexico v Cameroon, Group A — ITV, 5pm
Spain v Holland, Group B — BBC, 8pm
Chile v Australia, Group B — ITV, 11pm

JUNE 14
Colombia v Greece, Group C — BBC, 5pm
Uruguay v Costa Rica, Group D — ITV, 8pm
England v Italy, Group D — BBC, 11pm

JUNE 15
Ivory Coast v Japan, Group C — ITV, 2am
Switzerland v Ecuador, Group E — ITV, 5pm
France v Honduras, Group E — BBC, 8pm
Argentina v Bosnia-Herz., Group F — BBC, 11pm

JUNE 16
Germany v Portugal, Group G — ITV, 5pm
Iran v Nigeria, Group F — BBC, 8pm
Ghana v USA, Group G — BBC, 11pm

JUNE 17
Belgium v Algeria, Group H — ITV, 5pm
Brazil v Mexico, Group A — BBC, 8pm
Russia v South Korea, Group H — BBC, 11pm

JUNE 18
Australia v Holland, Group B — ITV, 5pm
Spain v Chile, Group B — BBC, 8pm
Cameroon v Croatia, Group A — ITV, 11pm

JUNE 19
Colombia v Ivory Coast, Group C — BBC, 5pm
Uruguay v England, Group D — ITV, 8pm
Japan v Greece, Group C — BBC, 11pm

JUNE 20
Italy v Costa Rica, Group D — BBC, 5pm
Switzerland v France, Group E — ITV, 8pm
Honduras v Ecuador, Group E — ITV, 11pm

JUNE 21
Argentina v Iran, Group F — ITV, 5pm
Germany v Ghana, Group G — BBC, 8pm
Nigeria v Bosnia-Herz., Group F — BBC, 11pm

JUNE 22
Belgium v Russia, Group H — BBC, 5pm
South Korea v Algeria, Group H — ITV, 8pm
USA v Portugal, Group G — BBC, 11pm

JUNE 23
Australia v Spain, Group B — ITV, 5pm
Holland v Chile, Group B — ITV, 5pm
Cameroon v Brazil, Group A — ITV, 9pm
Croatia v Mexico, Group A — ITV, 9pm

JUNE 24
Costa Rica v England, Group D — ITV, 5pm
Italy v Uruguay, Group D — ITV, 5pm
Greece v Ivory Coast, Group C — BBC, 9pm
Japan v Colombia, Group C — BBC, 9pm

JUNE 25
Bosnia-Herz. v Iran, Group F — ITV, 5pm
Nigeria v Argentina, Group F — ITV, 5pm
Ecuador v France, Group E — BBC, 9pm
Honduras v Switzerland, Group E — BBC, 9pm

JUNE 26
Portugal v Ghana, Group G — BBC, 5pm
USA v Germany, Group G — BBC, 5pm
Algeria v Russia, Group H — ITV, 9pm
South Korea v Belgium, Group H — ITV, 9pm

TURN OVER FOR MORE GAMES!

IT'S KNOCKOUT TIME!
The world's best 16 teams go head-to-head in the knockout stages!

LAST 16

GROUP A WINNER	**GROUP B RUNNER-UP**	**GROUP C WINNER**	**GROUP D RUNNER-UP**
MATCH 49	June 28 ★ 5pm TBC ★ Mineirao Stadium	**MATCH 50**	June 28 ★ 9pm TBC ★ Maracana Stadium
GROUP B WINNER	**GROUP A RUNNER-UP**	**GROUP D WINNER**	**GROUP C RUNNER-UP**
MATCH 51	June 29 ★ 5pm TBC ★ Castelao Stadium	**MATCH 52**	June 29 ★ 9pm TBC ★ Pernambuco Arena
GROUP E WINNER	**GROUP F RUNNER-UP**	**GROUP G WINNER**	**GROUP H RUNNER-UP**
MATCH 53	June 30 ★ 5pm TBC ★ Mane Garrincha	**MATCH 54**	June 30 ★ 9pm TBC ★ Beira-Rio Stadium
GROUP F WINNER	**GROUP E RUNNER-UP**	**GROUP H WINNER**	**GROUP G RUNNER-UP**
MATCH 55	July 1 ★ 5pm TBC ★ Sao Paulo Arena	**MATCH 56**	July 1 ★ 9pm TBC ★ Fonte Nova Arena

QUARTER-FINALS

MATCH 53 WINNER	**MATCH 54 WINNER**	**MATCH 49 WINNER**	**MATCH 50 WINNER**
MATCH 58	July 4 ★ 5pm TBC ★ Maracana Stadium	**MATCH 57**	July 4 ★ 9pm TBC ★ Castelao Stadium
MATCH 55 WINNER	**MATCH 56 WINNER**	**MATCH 51 WINNER**	**MATCH 52 WINNER**
MATCH 60	July 5 ★ 5pm TBC ★ Mane Garrincha	**MATCH 59**	July 5 ★ 9pm TBC ★ Fonte Nova Arena

SEMI-FINALS

MATCH 57 WINNER	**MATCH 58 WINNER**	**MATCH 59 WINNER**	**MATCH 60 WINNER**
MATCH 61	July 8 ★ 9pm TBC ★ Mineirao Stadium	**MATCH 62**	July 9 ★ 9pm TBC ★ Sao Paulo Arena

THIRD PLACE PLAY-OFF

MATCH 61 LOSER		**MATCH 62 LOSER**
MATCH 63	July 12 ★ 9pm TBC ★ Mane Garrincha Stadium	

THE FINAL

MATCH 61 WINNER		**MATCH 62 WINNER**
MATCH 64	July 13 ★ 8pm TBC ★ Maracana Stadium	

DAY-BY-DAY GUIDE!

LAST 16

JUNE 28
Group A Winner v Group B Runner-up	TBC, 5pm	
Group C Winner v Group D Runner-up	TBC, 9pm	

JUNE 29
Group B Winner v Group A Runner-up	TBC, 5pm	
Group D Winner v Group C Runner-up	TBC, 9pm	

JUNE 30
Group E Winner v Group F Runner-up	TBC, 5pm	
Group G Winner v Group H Runner-up	TBC, 9pm	

JULY 1
Group F Winner v Group E Runner-up	TBC, 5pm	
Group H Winner v Group G Runner-up	TBC, 9pm	

QUARTER-FINALS

JULY 4
Match 53 Winner v Match 54 Winner	TBC, 5pm	
Match 49 Winner v Match 50 Winner	TBC, 9pm	

JULY 5
Match 55 Winner v Match 56 Winner	TBC, 5pm	
Match 51 Winner v Match 52 Winner	TBC, 9pm	

SEMI-FINALS

JULY 8
Match 57 Winner v Match 58 Winner	TBC, 9pm	

JULY 9
Match 59 Winner v Match 60 Winner	TBC, 9pm	

THIRD PLACE PLAY-OFF

JULY 12
Match 61 Loser v Match 62 Loser	TBC, 9pm	

THE FINAL

JULY 13
Match 61 Winner v Match 62 Winner	TBC, 8pm	

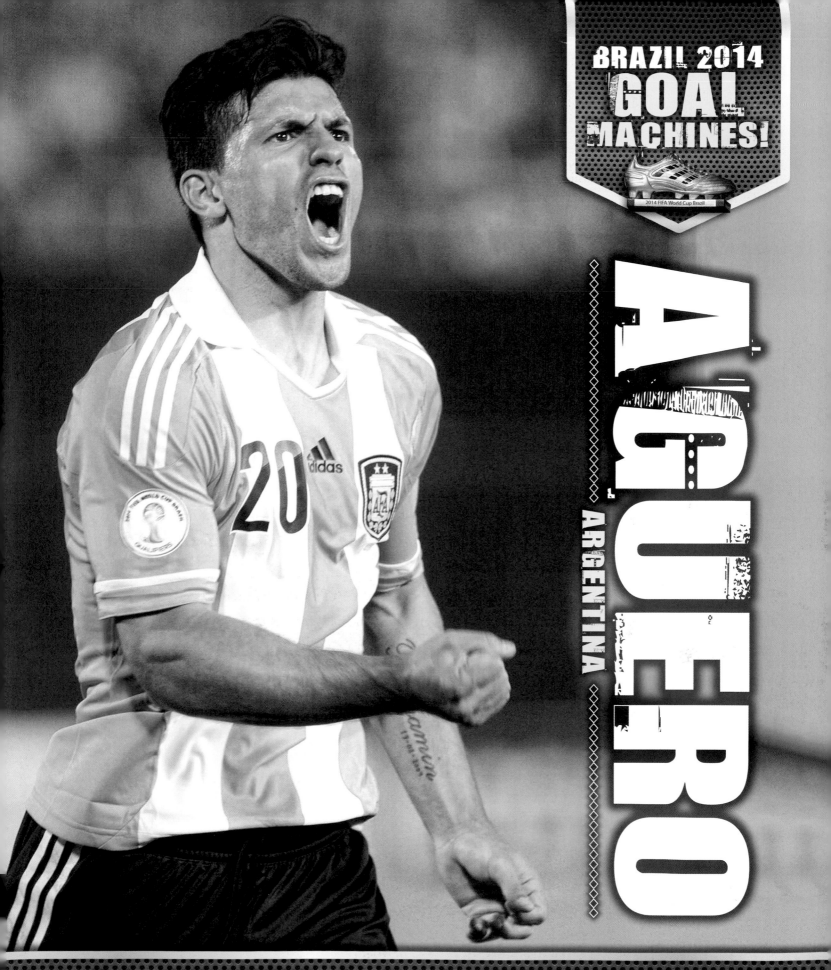

AGÜERO

ARGENTINA

Kun scored both goals as Argentina beat their opening 2014 World Cup opponents Bosnia 2-0 in a friendly in the USA last November!

Four of Aguero's five World Cup qualifying goals came against South American qualifiers Ecuador, Colombia and Uruguay!

The unstoppable Man. City goal machine has won the Olympics and two Under-20 World Cups with Argentina! What a ledge!

QUIZ ANSWERS!

Mega Quiz 1!   P.34-35

Camera Shy: Cristiano Ronaldo, Karim Benzema & Per Mertesacker.

Bogus Badge: Spain.

World Cup Heroes: Belgium - Kevin Mirallas; Ecuador - Antonio Valencia; Nigeria - Victor Moses.

Bonkers Fans: Holland.

Who Am I?: Edin Dzeko.

Name The Team: 1. Daniel Sturridge; 2. Danny Welbeck; 3. Phil Jagielka; 4. Joe Hart; 5. Gary Cahill; 6. Andros Townsend; 7. Wayne Rooney; 8. Steven Gerrard; 9. Michael Carrick; 10. Leighton Baines.

Footy Crazy: Teamgeist - 2006; Brazuca - 2014; Jabulani - 2010; Fevernova - 2002.

Mystery Mascot: France.

Flashback: Andres Iniesta.

Big Ten 1!   P.46

1. Twice; 2. A Lion – Cameroon's full nickname is The Indomitable Lions; 3. New York Red Bulls; 4. £11 million; 5. Chelsea; 6. Mario Mandzukic; 7. True; 8. Gregory van der Wiel; 9. 32 years old; 10. Sergio Busquets - he was 21 years old.

Spot The Stars!   P.56

1. Zlatan Ibrahimovic; 2. Gareth Bale; 3. Theo Walcott; 4. Aaron Ramsey; 5. Bryan Oviedo; 6. Branislav Ivanovic; 7. Christian Eriksen; 8. Seamus Coleman; 9. Scott Brown; 10. Jonny Evans.

Big Ten 2!   P.66

1. None; 2. Spain; 3. France; 4. Ecuador; 5. Roma; 6. Victor Moses; 7. 1986; 8. Diego Maradona; 9. Man. United; 10. Asmir Begovic.

Mega Quiz 2!   P.76-77

MATCH Winner: Jermain Defoe.

Sergio Aguero Quiz:
1. Independiente; 2. True; 3. £38 million; 4. Lionel Messi; 5. 26 years old.

FIFA 14 Challenge:
1. Eden Hazard; 2. Cesar Azpilicueta.

Soccer Scrabble: Robin van Persie.

Spot The Ball: B7.

Stadium Game: Manaus - England; Maracana - Argentina; Salvador - Spain; Porto Alegre - France.

True Or False?: 1. False - they've won it five times; 2. False - it was hosted in South Korea and Japan; 3. True; 4. True; 5. False - Spain beat Holland 1-0.

Wordsearch!   P.80

One point for each correct answer!

MY SCORE   /104

RONALDO

PORTUGAL

The Portugal megastar was the top scorer in last season's Champions League with 12 goals in 12 games for Real Madrid!

Ronaldo scored eight goals in the World Cup 2014 qualifiers, including all four in the two-legged play-off win over Sweden!

The forward hit his 400th career goal for club and country in just his 653rd game with a strike for Real Madrid against Celta Vigo in January 2014!

100% FOOTY ACTION EVERY WEEK!

MATCH!

LUIS' DECEMBER DOUBLE

RECORD BREAKER!

THE BIGGEST STARS!

AGUERO & NEGREDO!

MATCH BUILDS THE... ULTIMATE PLAYER!

AWESOME FEATURES!

f LIKE MATCH AT... FACEBOOK.COM/MATCHMAGAZINE f

100% FOOTY ACTION EVERY WEEK!

FIFA 14 TIPS & NEWS!

COOL FOOTY GEAR!

TOUGH QUIZZES!

EPIC POSTERS!

WIN TOP PRIZES!

CRAZY CARTOONS!

FUNNY PICS!

GET IT EVERY TUESDAY!

 FOLLOW MATCH AT... TWITTER.COM/MATCHMAGAZINE

MATCH! 93

MULLER
GERMANY

Muller netted a double against England at the last World Cup in 2010! He scored against Argentina, Australia and Uruguay too!

Muller hit eight goals in 12 starts - including strikes against Juventus, Barça and Arsenal - as Bayern won the Champions League in 2012-13!

The Germany superstar won the Golden Boot at World Cup 2010 after bagging five goals and three assists in South Africa!